THE FRENCH COURT

ESSAYS FROM ONE FAMILY'S LEGACY OF MENTAL ILLNESS

LAUREN HENRY BREHM

To my beloved daughter, R. A., who gave me the motivation to understand and overcome the legacy of The French Court.

And to all mental health care providers, everywhere, who help their clients heal from traumas large and small, especially those who helped me: Grace, Michael, Alan, Kelly, Cindy, Milan, Theresa, Susan, Heather, Isabella, and Bri.

CONTENTS

PREFACE

I wrote this book as a case study of my grandmother's experience with Obsessive-Compulsive Disorder (OCD). Her manifestation of this disease was unique; one of my own psychiatrists labeled it "OCD by Proxy." It is not a variation that exists in the fifth edition of the **Diagnostic and Statistical Manual of Mental Disorders** (DSM-5). It may never have existed before and may never appear again. There was a distinct confluence of factors that allowed my grandmother's manifestation to exist in the first place. It was a time when mental illness was stigmatized, so seeking help carried social risk if it was even available. It took OCD existing in someone who was strongwilled enough to seek control of others. It took a spouse who was unable to say "no" to his wife and unwilling or unable to protect his daughters from her. Above all, as I now suspect, it took a man who was willing to abuse his daughter and create the monster she became.

I started this project in 2003, interviewing several family members. After doing the background work and writing about 17,000 words, I let the project sit for twenty years, until the last of the principal characters died in 2023. I'm a bit protective of their memories, so there are no last names within. I've changed the first names of those who are still living to protect their privacy.

I also did a little bit of research when I started, partly about the nature of OCD itself, and, later, about incest survivors. As I assembled all the pieces of the puzzle from all of the different perspectives, I was struck by both my grandmother's and my mother's attitudes toward men. My grandmother was vocal about not valuing males—except for her father. My mother never stated a dislike of men, but was uninterested in sex. Her marriage to my father ended in part over issues of sexuality. Her closest male friends were gay men who were equally uninterested in a sexual relationship. It was easy to imagine my mother had picked up negative attitudes about men and sex from her mother, but I wanted to understand where her mother had acquired those attitudes. The essay titled "Victim" describes the moment my suspicions about incest were confirmed in my mind.

I am writing as if to a professional in the field because I think Grandma's story may contribute something to our understanding of OCD. I have chosen to write a series of essays rather than a narrative, but my grandmother's illness is the through line in all the essays. I wrote each essay separately from the others, so they overlap in some of the details. I have put them in an order that seems logical to me, but even so, the order is only slightly logical. Feel free to read them in any order you choose.

I am also writing for anyone who has someone in their family suffering from a mental illness. This isn't a book of advice—far from it! Do not do what my family did! It is, in most ways, a cautionary tale to be mindful. Mental illnesses happen, just as physical ones do. And, just as with physical illnesses, we have to protect mental illnesses from spreading to and harming others. The risk of contagion is high. The question for my family should have been how to treat the patient while protecting others from the effects of the illness, not how to keep the patient happy at any cost. Is the problem in my family genetic or environmental? I honestly don't know, nor do I think it matters. It has affected all subsequent generations thus far, however the legacy was transmitted.

Mostly, though, I am writing this for all twenty of my grand-mother's direct descendants to validate the family stories and memorialize our history before it fades into the past. It wasn't a nightmare. We lived it. We all bear the scars.

INTRODUCTION

I have a story to tell. I'm not sure whose story it is. It should be the story of my grandmother and her struggle with mental illness—Obsessive-Compulsive Disorder (OCD), to be specific. But my grandmother had a very strong personality, and her illness affected the people around her.

No. That's not quite accurate. That's like saying the Everglades are a little damp, or the Mona Lisa is a pretty painting. The vast understatement doesn't begin to convey the reality behind the seemingly innocuous sentence.

My grandmother was a cast iron bitch who so dominated her husband and daughters that she not only convinced them that her obsessive-compulsive routines and rituals were perfectly normal, but was able to bully them into taking part.

My father, who married into this insanity and made a quick exit six years later, often observed that there are two courses of action when someone is mentally ill enough to think they are Napoleon. The first is to secure appropriate treatment, so with therapy, medication, and time, the person can come to understand they are not, in fact, Napoleon, and can be returned to their own identity and a productive role in society. The second course of action is to set up a French court and indulge the person's fantasy of being Napoleon by changing reality to match the delusion.

My family chose the latter path.

At the time, it probably seemed to be the path of least resistance. It was much easier than standing up to the cast iron bitch. No one knew how to tell her "No." But now I don't know whose story I have to tell. Grandma was only the first victim of her own mental illness and its causes. She became the victimizer, first by abusing her husband and her daughters—my mother and aunt— whose childhoods were darkened by the growing shadow of their mother's encroaching mental illness, and whose adolescence and adulthood bore the full brunt of insanity in bloom. Eventually, she abused her grandchildren. None of the descendants have escaped. Three generations have been scarred by the illness of a single person. The jury is still out on the fourth generation.

I have a story to tell. I just don't know whose it is.

MEMORIES

My earliest memory is of being in the backyard of my house. I feel the warmth of the sun on my head and face, but it's not uncomfortably hot. I'm in a field a little beyond our yard itself. The weeds and flowers are taller than my head. I see bees buzzing lazily among the weeds at just about my eye level. I'm not afraid of the bees. In my memory, I don't even have a word for the creatures, though looking back at it, I know what I'm seeing are bees. My mother calls my name, and I return to our yard. End of memory.

One time we were talking about early memories, and I told my dad about this one. I also told him my mother had said it couldn't have happened because there was no such field. He shook his head and said my memory was better than hers. There was a field, just as I described, behind the house we lived in when my brother was born. We moved there when I was fifteen months old and moved out when I was three. The memory is from the warm season that first year, when I was sixteen to twenty-one months old.

I tell you this so you can have confidence in my childhood

memories. When I say I'm not sure about a memory, I mean it. But when I say I remember a thing, I mean that, too. You can trust my memories.

CHOKE AND DIE

THE HOUSE THAT OCD BUILT

Grandma Jean was afraid that she would choke and die. Grandma Jean was afraid that her mouth would dry out, and she would choke and die.

Grandma Jean would not permit salt in her house because she was afraid that salt would dry out her mouth, and she would choke and die.

Grandma Jean was afraid that she would get sick and have to take medicine, which would cause her mouth to dry out, and she would choke and die.

Grandma Jean washed her hands constantly, so she wouldn't get sick and have to take medicine, which would cause her mouth to dry out, and she would choke and die.

Grandma Jean's hands became bloody and raw from her constantly washing them, so she wouldn't get sick and have to take medicine, which would cause her mouth to dry out, and she would choke and die.

Grandma Jean always wore two pairs of black cotton gloves so her hands wouldn't get bloody and raw from washing them, so she wouldn't get sick and have to take medicine, which would cause her mouth to dry out, and she would choke and die.

Grandma Jean always wore two pairs of black cotton gloves, so she wouldn't feel the need to wash her hands, but this made it impossible for her to handle or prepare food, so she made the person who prepared her food wash their hands in front of her, so she wouldn't get sick and have to take medicine, which would cause her mouth to dry out, and she would choke and die.

Grandma Jean temporarily lost the ability to taste food due to a cold and became afraid she might become sick from eating bad food and have to take medicine, which would cause her mouth to dry out, and she would choke and die.

Grandma Jean decided eggs, because they are in a shell, and bread, fresh from the bakery, from the center of the loaf, with the crusts cut off, were safe, sterile foods to eat, even for someone who couldn't taste food due to a cold, and therefore not likely to make her sick, and have to take medicine, which would cause her mouth to dry out, and she would choke and die.

Grandma Jean lived for over forty years on a diet of eggs, bread, and coffee that was made in a drip coffee maker in front of her, so she could watch. For even longer than that, she wore two pairs of black cotton gloves at all times—plus a coat and a hat—to protect her from germs, so she wouldn't get sick, and have to take medicine, which would cause her mouth to dry out, and she would choke and die.

The official cause of death listed on Grandma Jean's death certificate was "dehydration." Her mouth dried out, and she choked and died. She was ninety-five.

OBSESSIVE-COMPULSIVE DISORDER

The **Diagnostic and Statistical Manual of Mental Disorders, Fifth Edition Text Revision**, published by the American Psychiatric Association in 2022, is more commonly known as the DSM-5. This 1050-page volume is the final word in defining what constitutes a mental illness, a veritable bible setting forth the rules by which practitioners diagnose their patients.

The DSM-5 lists the criteria for Obsessive-Compulsive Disorder.[1] Obsessions are "recurrent and persistent thoughts, urges, or images that are ... intrusive and unwanted ... (and that) the individual attempts to ignore or suppress...." Compulsions are "repetitive behaviors that the individual feels driven to perform in response to an obsession or according to rules that must be applied rigidly." Although the person is doing these things to reduce their anxiety, the acts are not related to the object of their obsession "or are clearly excessive." OCD behaviors are time consuming, taking up more than an hour a day. The

---

1. American Psychiatric Association (2022). *Diagnostic and Statistical Manual of Mental Disorders* (5th ed., p. 265). American Psychiatric Association Publishing.

behaviors cannot be the result of some other physical or mental health condition nor the result of substance abuse.

Within the disorder are several subtypes having to do with the degree of insight the patient has about the reality of their obsessions and compulsions. Grandma Jean firmly believed there was nothing wrong with her and those who thought there was something wrong were crazy themselves. That characteristic suggests her full diagnosis was "Obsessive-Compulsive Disorder absent insight with delusional beliefs."[2]

My grandmother was diagnosed with OCD. I don't know when she was diagnosed or by whom. It wasn't when she went to Philadelphia in 1942, a year after the death of her beloved father, to visit her married sister and her physician husband. At the time, Jean couldn't stop crying and washing her hands. She and her daughters, nine year old Anita (my mother) and twelve year old Mary (my aunt), went for a "visit"; in reality, she was consulting a psychiatrist, but doing so where she wouldn't experience the stigma that accompanied seeking mental health treatment. At that time, the doctor diagnosed early-onset menopause; essentially, Jean was suffering from "female troubles" or hysteria. She was thirty-four.

She may have been diagnosed with OCD the time she was carted off to Bellevue Hospital in 1946. In that event, Grandpa Bob had run away from home. He did this at least three times that I know of. Anita and Mary were thirteen and sixteen respectively when their father left the first time.[3] With Bob gone, Jean became frantic. The girls couldn't calm her and didn't know what else to do, so they called for help. An ambulance from Bellevue hospital came, and the attendants took Jean away. I don't have any information about her hospital stay, but it seems likely that

---

2. Ibid, p. 266
3. The second time was during my parents' engagement, while the third was when I was around nine. I only know about the last time because I happened to answer the phone when Grandpa called to check on the family.

was when her behaviors were analyzed and the diagnosis of Obsessive-Compulsive Disorder was first applied.

Anita was happy to have her mother out of the house, but Mary was wracked with guilt. As the older girl, she was the one who had made the decision to call for help, and she felt responsible for what had happened to her mother. I was already the mother of a school-aged child when I had lunch with both my mother and my aunt, and this topic came up. From the information exchanged, I gathered the conversation represented the first time the two sisters—after over fifty years—had ever talked about the incident and how they each felt about it. Grandma's problems were rarely discussed in our family, though they weren't treated as secrets. Her illness was so normalized and accepted in the family that talking about it seemed somehow irrelevant, like a fish asking, "What water?"

Regardless of where and when Jean was diagnosed, everyone around her knew what Obsessive-Compulsive Disorder was. Every member of her family down to her grandchildren could give a lecture on the disease; we were all intimately acquainted with the symptoms of OCD.

After Jean's experience with the psychiatrist in Philadelphia, she decided doctors didn't know anything and wouldn't voluntarily see one again unless someone insisted on it. My mother absorbed Jean's distrust of medical practice. That may be part of why she resisted taking my brother and me to doctors and dentists.

I don't know what Jean's obsessions were beyond the obvious fear of getting sick. The list of her compulsions could fill a book.

GRANDMA JEAN AND GRANDPA BOB

When Grandma Jean was six years old, she resisted going to school on her first day. Her mother, my great-grandmother, walked her to the school, with little Jean crying and protesting the whole way. Jean wasn't a particularly clingy child, but she was uncomfortable in new situations. She preferred the familiar. Great-grandma Leah dropped her crying daughter off at the school. By the time Leah returned to her home, Jean was already there. She had run away from the school as soon as she could. That is the earliest story that demonstrates my grandmother's emotional problems and her strong will. It serves now as foreshadowing for the rest of Jean's life.

In 1920-something, my great-grandparents were having trouble with Jean. The exact nature of that trouble hasn't been recorded for posterity, so I can't say whether she was showing signs of a nervous disorder or if she was being headstrong. Either would be possible. In any event, they sent Jean from Philadelphia, Pennsylvania, to Atlantic City, New Jersey, to live with her married sister Rose. Rose was working in a plumber's office and got Jean a job there. After some months, Rose got a better job in another office. As Rose was planning to leave, Jean cried inconsolably and begged her to stay. Jean was afraid of staying in the old job without her sister nearby.

Jean's brother Max was also in Atlantic City, working for an insurance company. He introduced Jean to one of his colleagues. Robert was a former Merchant Marine from Brooklyn, New York, where his father owned a butcher shop. Jean and Bob dated for a while, and he asked for her hand in marriage. Jean's family was against the marriage. Her parents tried to talk Bob out of marrying Jean because she was such a difficult young woman to deal with. Again, it is not clear if they were basing this judgment on her strong-willed nature or some other behavior. However, Jean's family clearly did not believe Bob was up to the task of handling Jean. In hindsight, it seems they were correct.

Bob and Jean were married in June, 1929. Their first daughter, Mary, was born in March, 1930. Their second daughter, Anita, my mother, was born in February, 1933. Both girls were born in Atlantic City. When Anita was eight months old, the family relocated to Brooklyn. Bob was no longer able to make a living working in insurance due to the Depression. His father Abraham employed an assistant in his butcher shop. He fired the assistant to give the position to his son. Bob eventually inherited the family business, although he had never intended to follow in his father's footsteps.

Jean was always in charge of the family. While Bob may have been the provider outside the home, Jean determined what the family would do and how and when. In part, this may have been a function of intellect; Jean was by far the more intelligent of the two. However, the dynamic of family leadership was mostly a function of temperament. Jean was domineering, while Bob was placid. Even without mental illness factoring into the situation, Jean would have been an authoritarian wife and mother while Bob would have been a compliant husband. The Yiddish word *nebbish*, meaning a person of no significance, could have been invented to describe my grandfather, except he wasn't important enough to have prompted its coinage.

Jean's obsessive-compulsive behaviors started at some point after her father's death in 1941 with handwashing. At that time, her daughters were eight and eleven. She would stand at the bathroom sink and wash her hands repeatedly. Her hands were never clean enough, so she could never stop washing. One evening, Bob went into the bathroom and turned off the water to force her to stop. That was the first link in the chain that bound him to Jean's routines for the rest of their lives. Each night thereafter, Jean would call for Bob to come and turn off the water. Someone other than Jean had to control her behavior, though she in turn controlled the person who controlled her behavior. Bob's docile nature made it easy for Jean to manipulate him into doing what she wanted.

Sometimes Bob would feel overwhelmed with the prison he existed in. He would sell part of his valuable coin collection and run away from home. He was a caring father, though, and always called home to check on his daughters. Jean would inevitably promise to change. Bob would believe her and come home, but nothing ever changed. The last time Grandpa Bob ran away from home, I answered the phone when he called my mother. I was sworn to secrecy lest Grandma Jean learn he had been in touch. My answering that call was the only reason I learned my grandfather had run away from home, a behavior usually associated with children.

Bob usually ran to Idlewood, the campground his sister Gert and her husband owned in the mountains around Hendersonville, North Carolina. The family took a rare vacation there in the 1940s, during the war. If the photos are an accurate record, the family of four—Bob, Jean, Mary, and Anita—enjoyed being there in one of the cabins.

Bob also ran to Idlewood during Anita and Hank's engagement. The family dispatched Anita to talk him into returning.

Hank either accompanied her to Hendersonville or met her there later. Anita warned Hank her family was crazy. Maybe he shouldn't marry her. Hank had had a front row seat to the family's way of dealing with Jean's problems. He thought he knew what he was marrying into. Hank reassured Anita that he loved her. He confided to me as an adult that he regretted not breaking off the engagement then. He had thought Anita's problems would resolve once she left her mother's home. They didn't.

Jean never approved of any of the boys her daughters dated. When Hank and Anita, the first of the daughters to marry, sought approval of their engagement, Jean was reluctant to grant permission. Her disapproval may have softened somewhat when I was born three years later. She doted on me. After all, I was a girl.

Jean had no use for men. Presumably she knew she needed one in order to have children and to function socially in that time. Beyond that, she thought men and boys were worthless. Jean attended a social event with my parents where there was a newborn baby boy in the household. The occasion was the baby's *bris*, the ritual circumcision of a Jewish male at eight days old. My father asked Jean if she intended to say something to the new parents. She replied that she never offered congratulations for boys.

The only man Grandma Jean ever considered worthwhile was her father, who was apparently a paragon of all manly virtues.

MY DINNER WITH GRANDMA

My grandmother came for a visit without my grandfather when I was in eighth grade. Grandpa Bob was having heart surgery out-of-state, with Aunt Mary accompanying him, so the family decided Grandma Jean needed to stay with my mother in North Carolina while her husband was unable to care for her. Grandma needed someone else to perform her routines, so if Grandpa wasn't available, one of her daughters had to step up.

One evening there was no one available to be Grandma's "keeper." That's the job title my then-boyfriend and I gave a few years later to the series of hired helpers who took care of Grandma's needs after she was widowed. My mother tried to find someone, paid or not, to be with Grandma Jean for her meal time rituals for that one night, roughly 5:00 to 8:00 in the evening. No one was available.

Grandma and Grandpa had always closed the kitchen doors for the whole three hours, even when they were not in the room. None of us were allowed to enter the kitchen during those times lest we contaminate the area. That meant we had to eat our own meal either very early or very late. By age thirteen, I was dying of curiosity to know what went on behind those closed doors. I had imagined all sorts of scenarios, from Grandpa grinding up Grandma's food and feeding it to her like a baby to magical incantations to make the food safe for consumption. I wanted to know what secrets lurked behind the doors. I volunteered to be Grandma's keeper for the evening.

The meal prep started at 5:00 when Grandma Jean took her wind-up clock into the kitchen to check the time against the electric wall clock and wind the clock. She took her regular three tablespoon dose of mineral oil at that time. My job was to pour the oil for her and hold the spoon to her lips. Grandma instructed me on how to perform her rituals, as well as the reasoning or rationale behind them. Not that reason or rationality had anything to do with it.

I got a short break until it was time to start preparing her meal. First, I had to wash my hands at the kitchen sink while Grandma Jean supervised me. She had her own special kitchen tools, plate, and cutlery. I took bread out of the package that had been bought earlier that day, skipping over the ends to take slices from the middle. I cut the crusts of bread off and threw them out. I cooked Grandma a scrambled egg and put it on her plate with the bread. Grandma stood over me, her hands behind her back, rocking, as I followed her instructions.

At the table, I folded a full-sized paper towel sheet into quarters, then slid the towel into Grandma's left hand between her thumb and forefinger which were encased, as always, in her black cotton gloves. Her other hand held a fork. I placed a slice of bread into the paper towel "claw." She used the bread to sweep the egg onto the fork. My job was to watch her eat, I assume to make sure she didn't choke on anything.

When Grandma finished her food, we drove to a diner where the coffee was made in a drip coffee maker so she could watch. Grandma Jean was the driver, even when Grandpa Bob was with her. Since she went to the diner at least twice a day, every day, the people at the counter knew her. They may have known she was odd, but she could be quite charming with people she didn't try to control, and they liked seeing her come in to chat and get a cup of coffee to go. In later years, especially after Grandpa was gone, we had a drip coffee maker at home, so the travel to and from the diner or coffee shop as part of the evening routine ended.

Grandma's coffee was black. We added milk and sugar at the table at home. Grandma asked repeatedly if the coffee had enough sugar. I wasn't sure how I was supposed to know since no one was tasting it, and I had no frame of reference for how sweet Grandma wanted it. I put in the first spoonful and stirred the coffee.

"Is it sweet enough?" Grandma asked.

"Yes."

"No, it's not. Put in another spoonful." I obeyed. "Is it sweet enough?"

I still didn't know, but I said it was.

"No, it's not. Put in more. Just the tip of the spoon." I dutifully complied. "Is it sweet enough?"

"Yes?" I was a little uncertain by now.

"No, it's not. Just a tip more."

And again. The same question, followed by ignoring my answer, and the request for "just a tip more." At some point, the coffee was deemed sweet enough, regardless of what I had said. Then we repeated the process with the milk. I wasn't sure why Grandma was asking for my opinion when she was going to ignore it anyway. When the coffee was judged correct, Grandma drank it. I cleaned up from the meal and washed the dishes.

The final task was washing out her mouth in the bathroom. She handed me her partial to wash in the sink with a toothbrush. She told me that when it was made, the dentist had told her to correct anyone who said she had a big mouth because her dentures were the smallest he'd ever made. I inwardly rolled my eyes. Grandma was a bully and a busybody who never held back an opinion. Did she have a big mouth? Oh, yes.

I gave her a glass of water. There was the same back and forth eyeballing the level of the water in the glass as we'd had with the sugar and the milk. Using a measuring cup and pouring the correct amount into the drinking glass would have made more sense, which might be why we were having to eyeball the water level in an unmarked glass. Logic was never part of Grandma's *modus operandi*. When I finally had the right amount of water in the glass, she drank it.

For a few hours on a weeknight when I was thirteen, I had the experience of being Grandma Jean's keeper and doing my grandmother's routines with and for her. I remain grateful the toileting routine wasn't part of my duties. In later years, I would witness parts of the same routines played out with various keepers. There was little, if any, variation. Every day. For forty years or more.

GRANDMA'S HANDS

I was forty years old the first time I saw my grandmother's hands. My daughter and I had gone to visit Grandma Jean at the nursing home after learning that she seemed to be declining. Rebecca had to miss a couple of days from school to make the trip. We got the absence excused by telling the principal we thought it was better for Rebecca to miss class to visit her great-grandmother while she was alive, which was normally not an excused absence, rather than wait for the funeral when the absence would be excused. In the event, Grandma Jean's death didn't take place for another three and a half years.

When we visited Grandma, she was nonverbal and incontinent, the result of cognitive decline and a series of mini strokes. She normally didn't recognize visitors, but she seemed to recognize Rebecca. Senility had in many ways been a blessing to Grandma. She had forgotten all her routines bit by bit. Her anxieties and compulsions had disappeared. She was just a little old lady, frail and white-haired, sitting in a wheel chair. For the first time in my life, I saw her hands uncovered.

Her hands were small and pink, with the tissue-paper-thin skin of extreme old age. She was ninety-two at the time. For all that Grandma Jean was an overpowering presence in the lives of her relatives, she was barely five feet tall. "Five-foot nuthin'" she would say, when asked her height. Her hands reflected her petite stature and delicate build.

Grandma's hands also reflected more than half a century of being swathed in cloth and protected from contact with the world. Her hands neither touched the outside world nor did any work in the world for at least the last fifty years of her life. Cotton gloves formed a barrier between Grandma's hands and the dangers of the world around her. In her mind, that barrier was impermeable to dirt and germs.

During one of my overnight visits to Grandma Jean and Grandpa Bob's house when I was young, I woke up early in the morning to use the bathroom. On my way back to bed, I noticed the door to Grandma's bedroom was ajar. I couldn't resist the temptation to peek in. There she was, asleep, her hands lightly resting on the quilt, the ubiquitous gloves on her hands. I wondered if there was some mystery about her hands that made her keep them hidden from view.

At age forty, I knew why she had kept her hands covered all those years, but I still couldn't help but search her hands for the answers they might hold. All I saw were delicate pink hands with smooth white nails. No scars or calluses. No roughened edges. No redness, arthritis, or other signs of aging. To me, those hands symbolized all the pain she had inflicted on her family, from the early days of washing them raw to figuratively ruling with an iron hand. She had held all our destinies in the palms of those hands lying limply on the blanket covering her lap. Those tiny, powerless, hands.

NATURE OR NURTURE

Nature or Nurture. That's the name scientists give to the debate over whether we are born with certain traits or whether we learn them. Will playing music for your unborn baby somehow turn her into a math genius? If you put a basketball into your toddler's hands early enough, could he be the next Michael Jordan? Or does the kid have to be born with some ability and no amount of talking into belly buttons or playing the right music is going to change destiny?

Those on the nurture side of the debate believe the right environment can shape a child into anyone or anything. Those on the nature side believe some traits are hard-wired into the human brain and cannot be changed. The prize for both camps is when they find a pair of identical twins who have been raised apart from each other, especially when they have been ignorant of each other's existence. These children share identical genetics, and therefore presumably the same wiring, but totally different environments.

Scientists study pairs of both identical and fraternal twins, raised apart or together, in order to determine the extent to which human traits are influenced by nature as opposed to nurture and vice versa. An Australian study published in 2015 drew on virtually every twin study done over a fifty-year span.[1] The meta-analysis of data derived from 2,748 studies documenting 14,558,903 pairs of twins showed that, on average, variations among humans are 49 per cent genetic, and 51 percent environmental. Interestingly, influences on some traits were not as evenly divided. For example, the risk for bipolar disorder was about 70 percent due to genetics and 30 percent due to environmental factors.

My own experience leads me to believe that when it comes to mental illness, it doesn't matter whether the cause is nature, from within the individual, or nurture, from within the environment. I was being evaluated for possible depression at the same time my four-year-old daughter was being evaluated for what appeared to be a self-esteem problem. I completed a self-reported personality inventory for myself on the same day I completed a parent-reported inventory for Rebecca.

Talk about guilt! Did she inherit it from me? Did I inflict it on her? How did this happen? Nature? Nurture? Then I realized it didn't matter. If my depression had a genetic cause, like a chemical imbalance, and I had passed it on to her, then I couldn't have prevented it except by not having given birth to her. If it was nature, I couldn't do anything about it. If I didn't pass it on to her genetically, then I still could be responsible by having raised her in an unhealthy environment. If it was nurture, well, what do you think is going to happen when a little girl is raised by a mentally ill mother?

Which really explains a lot about how my mother was raised, how she raised me, and how I raised Rebecca.

The jackpot nature versus nurture question is whether Jean

---

1. Meta-analysis of the heritability of human traits based on fifty years of twin studies" by Tinca J C Polderman, Beben Benyamin, Christiaan A de Leeuw, Patrick F Sullivan, Arjen van Bochoven, Peter M Visscher and Danielle Posthuma in *Nature Genetics*. Published online May 18 2015 doi:10.10.1038/ng.3285

would have abused her family, creating a mental illness incubator in her descendants, if she had not been abused herself.

VICTIM

I n <u>Secret Survivors: Uncovering Incest and Its Aftereffects in Women</u>, E. Sue Blume presents the Incest Survivors' Aftereffects Checklist. This inventory of thirty-four characteristics draws on Blume's experience as a private therapist to women who suffered sexual abuse in childhood at the hands of trusted caregivers and family members in order to itemize ways in which such abuse may manifest in adulthood.[1]

Grandma Jean is no longer here to be interviewed about the more internalized items on the checklist. For example, number 25 on the inventory says feeling crazy, feeling different, feeling oneself to be unreal, etc. Unless Jean told someone specifically she felt this way, there would be no record remaining. However, we do have the record of her behavior, through which we can infer a lot about what Jean thought and felt. Looking through the inventory, there are several items which indicate Jean may have been the victim of incest.

Item 2: Swallowing and gagging sensitivity

---

1. Bloom, E. S. (1990). *Secret Survivors: Uncovering Incest and Its Aftereffects in Women* (pp. xxvii-xxx). Ballantine.

We've already seen that many of Jean's compulsions had to do with her fear of choking.

Item 4: Gastrointestinal problems

Jean closely monitored what went into her digestive tract and what came out. Her mealtimes and toileting were highly ritualized. She was obsessed with whether or not her bowel movements were normal. She took mineral oil every day on a rigid schedule to keep her bowel habits regular.

Item 5: Wearing a lot of clothing, even in summer

Jean wore two pairs of gloves, a hat, and a coat at all times, regardless of the time of year, indoors and out. Ostensibly this was to protect her from germs and contamination. She may also have used the extra clothing to conceal her body.

Item 6: Eating disorders; compulsive behaviors

Jean's entire meal regimen was an eating disorder and certainly a set of compulsive behaviors. Jean's behaviors may not be classic examples of overeating or self-starvation disorders, but they certainly fit the description of "eating disorders."

Item 7: Suicidal thoughts, attempts, obsession

Jean frequently expressed the wish to be dead, but she, like Hamlet, was afraid of what might come next. She would make threats to kill herself without ever having any intention of carrying them out.

One morning, my mother was preparing Grandma's breakfast. Grandma Jean was about seventy-five. She thought my mother was being unsympathetic to her perceived needs. Grandma reached suddenly for the butter knife and held it to her own throat, threatening to kill herself with it. My mother sighed and waited for her mother to stop being so dramatic. I was around twenty-four, visiting my mother and grandmother. I sat silently, looking from one woman to the other, ready to intervene if necessary. Eventually, realizing her audience wasn't buying her performance, my grandmother put the knife down and continued eating breakfast. Later, I saw there was a tiny scratch on her neck from the edge of the butter knife. She had held the knife close enough to her skin to nick herself, and it still hadn't cut her. I realized Grandma had known exactly what she was doing when she threatened to kill herself with a knife that couldn't possibly hurt her.

Item 11: Depression, seemingly baseless crying

When Jean was thirty-four, she and her daughters were sent to Philadelphia so Jean could see a psychiatrist. The reason for this was that Jean could not stop crying. The putative reason for the crying was the early onset of menopause, but I have to question if this was really the case. Doctors of the time (circa 1942) may well have called it hysteria, or ascribed it to "female troubles," but that need not have been an accurate diagnosis given the medical prejudices of the time. Jean had a sister in Philadelphia who had married a doctor and could presumably get her in to see a psychiatrist without having any stigma attached. Jean went to a couple of appointments and then refused to go back.

It is worth noting that this uncontrolled and baseless crying began the year after Morris, the father Jean worshipped, died.

Item 12: Anger issues; intense hostility toward entire gender or ethnic group of the perpetrator.

Jean hated all men with one exception: she idolized her father. He alone, of all males, was singled out for special status. Was he different from all other males because he was the one male who sexually abused Jean? Yet, if he was the perpetrator, why would Jean then put him on a pedestal?

Blume gives us some insight into Jean's possible thought processes. By blaming herself for the abuse and casting herself as a "bad" person, Jean would have been able to keep her image of her father pure and untarnished.[2] Any child, even one who is suffering incestuous abuse at the hands of a parent, is dependent on that parent for care, clothing, food, and shelter. For that

---

2. Ibid, p. 114.

parent to be untrustworthy is for the child to risk abandonment, starvation, and death. The fact Morris was the only male Jean considered praiseworthy makes it that much more likely he was the perpetrator of her abuse.

Item 18: Boundary issues; control, power, territoriality issues; fear of losing control; obsessive-compulsive behaviors

Blume observes that "the incest experience represents abuses of power and loss of control."[3] Victims of incest have often given up part of their personhood in acceding to the desires of someone else without having a choice in the matter. They feel as if they are themselves merely an extension of that other person. In adulthood, they may feel that they have to do what is asked of them without having the right to decline. They may develop boundary issues, having difficulty recognizing where one person ends and another begins. This lack of personhood means they may surrender power and control over their own lives to others.

Jean reacted to the loss of power and control she suffered from abuse by claiming all the power and control in her other relationships. Since her own boundaries were not respected, she didn't know how to respect the boundaries of other people. She didn't understand where she ended and others began and therefore tried, successfully, to control the other members of her immediate family.

Certainly, Jean exhibited obsessive-compulsive behaviors. Handwashing. Rocking. Food rituals. Toilet rituals. Checking.

Let me reiterate that there may be other items on the checklist that would emerge as applicable to Jean if she were here to be interviewed. Obviously, she isn't here, so I can only comment on those items where there is a record of observable behavior.

I read Blume's book because after interviewing family members and doing some initial research, I was starting to suspect Jean had been the victim of incest. I was especially suspi-

---

3. Ibid, p. 34

cious about why she idolized her father, who was by all accounts a meek tailor, but hated all other men. I was looking for clues toward verification.

When I first read the checklist, sitting in a college library, tears came to my eyes. It was the first time I saw Jean as a victim instead of a victimizer. Even though I'm a progressive liberal, I don't believe being a victim excuses you from responsibility for your actions. If anything, being a victim should make you more aware of the harm you cause others. Still, imagining Grandma Jean as a little girl, suffering abuse at the hands of the man who should have been protecting her, made me cry for the girl she was and the woman she could have been.

THE LEGACY OF THE FRENCH COURT

I don't want to put myself in the role of diagnosing mental illnesses or unusual tendencies in others because I'm not qualified to do so, nor do I necessarily know my family members well enough to know what goes on inside their heads. I can only observe the outward behaviors and describe them. I also know about some formal diagnoses because the information was shared among the family.

Grandma Jean bequeathed a legacy of mental illness and addictions to each of her descendants. It doesn't matter if the inheritance came through our genes or because a mentally ill parent created a toxic environment. The first two generations all carried the burden she left us. Among the seven members of those generations are six past or present tobacco smokers, four who drink/drank alcohol on a daily basis, and three who are/were daily users of cannabis. Only two are known to have sought therapy.

My own diagnoses include an Autism Spectrum Disorder (ASD) and dysthymia—chronic, low-level depression—marked with periods of major depression. I see in myself indications of

Obsessive-Compulsive Personality, though some of that may be secondary to my autism. People with both conditions find comfort in daily, predictable routines.

In terms of educationally related diagnoses, among those seven are speech impairments, learning disabilities, and autism. I suspect attention deficit/hyperactivity disorder is also among our problems, but I'm not sure it has ever been diagnosed. We were born in the 1930s and 1960s, when ADHD, autism, and learning disabilities weren't well-defined or recognized. It's reasonable to conclude some educational diagnoses were missed.

In addition to substance use/abuse, there are other addictive behaviors in those two generations. I have morbid obesity. That may be related in part to genetics; I have the same shape as my grandfather and my mother. However, I also have a sugar addiction and overeating disorder. Another member of these generations had an addiction to religion, going from the secular upbringing all of us had to a family life that valued religious adherence above all else.

All of the first seven of Grandma's descendants were married; six were divorced. Three of the marriages lasted over twenty-five years, while two of the marriages lasted less than a year. Only one of those who divorced has remarried. I don't know to what extent the marital failures were due to not having good role models of what a happy, functional marriage looks like. Jean and Bob's marriage wasn't a good role model. Neither was Hank and Anita's. Mary and her husband kept their vows "'til death do us part," but I wouldn't describe their marriage as "functional." As one of my cousins put it, "It's amazing how close we are considering how fucked-up our family is." My marriage, which lasted the longest among my generation at twenty-nine years, probably thrived for so long because my husband and I explicitly looked to my father and stepmother's marriage as a model for ourselves. There were times when we were problem solving and asked ourselves "What would Mom and Dad do?"

Grandma Jean demanded a clean and uncluttered house in keeping with her fear of germs, though she played no role in keeping the house up to her standards. Mary absorbed her mother's standards, though not her illness, and also demanded a clean home. Anita, in contrast, had hoarding tendencies. Her home was always cluttered and dirty. She also allowed her floors and furniture to double as toilet areas for her pet dogs and cats. Her personal hygiene was dismal. She rarely bathed or showered. She didn't brush her teeth regularly until later in life when she developed gum disease. My mother seemed almost the opposite of obsessive-compulsive, at least when it came to cleanliness.

Mother's standards for some things were unrealistically high. Although she taught young children, primarily kindergarten, she wasn't able to see me through a developmentally appropriate lens and always demanded more than I was capable of doing. The most obvious example of her skewed expectations occurred when I took a one hundred item test as part of the admission process for graduate school. I scored eighty-three correct. When I told my mother how I had done, she asked if I had missed the other items because I didn't have enough time to finish, implying there must have been a reason for me not to have a perfect score other than simply getting them wrong. On another occasion, I told her my psychiatrist had asked me why I was a perfectionist. She asked if I had told him it was because my mother was perfect. I suspect she meant that as a joke, but I didn't find it funny.

According to the DSM-5, perfectionism is a trait of Obsessive-Compulsive Personality Disorder (771). While most people who show perfectionistic traits constantly pursue perfection, some react to having impossibly high standards by not trying to reach those standards at all. Thus, someone who is messy and sloppy may be a perfectionist, but reacts to high expectations by not trying to meet them. My daughter's inability to practice developmental skills, like music or sports, with the inherent message that practicing meant she wasn't already perfect, was an example of that mindset, as was my mother's inability to keep herself and her home at a minimal level of cleanliness. The thinking behind that is "if I don't try, I can't fail." Other traits of Obsessive-Compulsive Personality Disorder relate to a need for control. The DSM-5 includes diagnostic criteria that suggest someone who is inflexible, unable to compromise their standards in order to work with others, rigid, stubborn, and has a tendency toward hoarding (772). Among Grandma Jean's first seven descendants are at least five, myself included, who have been accused of being controlling by other family members. None of us have had models of how to respect other people's boundaries. It is not difficult to imagine that Grandma's need for control as a consequence of being abused created a similar need for control in those whose lives were controlled or impacted by Grandma Jean's behavior.

Of course, Obsessive-Compulsive Personality Disorder includes other criteria, so recognizing some characteristics is not confirmation of having that disorder. The fact that Mary kept a spotlessly clean home and Anita kept a hopelessly filthy one shows their reactions to their mother's OCD, but does not constitute a clear pattern or diagnosis.

The eleven members of the third generation in descent from Grandma Jean currently range in age from eighteen to forty. Some have not shown any signs of mental illness, but that sadly doesn't mean they won't. Among the DSM-5 diagnoses that are known in that generation are anxiety, depression, bipolar disorder, attention deficit/hyperactivity disorder, and autism spectrum disorder. There are likely some addictions or other issues in that group as well, but the only one I can confirm is one daily user of cannabis.

All of the illnesses and addictions I've mentioned are common and appear in many families. The thing that stands out to me is the percentage of family members affected. Grandma Jean's mental illness seems to have affected 100% of her first- and second-generation descendants. That seems like an unusually high percentage. Even by the third generation, about half of the family members have problems that are found in the DSM-5.

Mental illness doesn't run in my family; it gallops.

SHIT

My mother had a problem with shit.

Her definition of paper training a puppy was to have enough newspaper on the floor that wherever the dog went to the bathroom was on the paper. Rather than using paper training as a transitional step in teaching the dog to go outside, she used the paper as an end in itself. The net result was her floors were covered with dog shit, albeit on paper, all the time.

My mother got a French poodle puppy, Napoleon, shortly after I was born. There were other dogs during her brief marriage to my father, but Napoleon stayed with her even after the divorce. When I was nine, she decided to get a beagle puppy. Our apartment was carpeted in newspapers so Ottavio, the puppy, would have some place to go. My mother would just leave the soiled newspapers sitting there. The turds would get hard and start to turn white before anyone would ever clean them up. I thought everyone in New York apartments who had dogs had yellow newspapers and dog turds in their living room, just like we did.

When we moved to North Carolina, the dogs had a yard to

relieve themselves in. The newspapers disappeared, but the shit didn't. The dogs thought nothing of lifting their legs against the furniture or squatting in the living room. Cats were added to the mix. They were indoor/outdoor cats, so presumably they went to the bathroom outside, but they also had an indoor litter box. However, my mother cleaned the litter box so rarely the cats wouldn't use it. They joined the dogs in shitting all over the house. One time, a visiting friend who was in a sleeping bag on the floor in the living room woke up to find cat shit in her hair. Needless to say, she rushed to the shower immediately.

My mother wasn't bothered by all this shit. She seemed not to notice it. According to my father, she also didn't notice it when she changed the diapers of her babies and left the soiled cloth diapers in the toilet. According to my aunt, she didn't notice it when she let my brother sit in his own soiled diaper rather than change it. And I know that when I let her babysit for my infant daughter, she let my daughter cry herself to sleep rather than change her soiled diaper, and then claimed Rebecca must have soiled herself in her sleep. I returned home to find my daughter asleep, her cheeks flushed from crying, her damp hair matted to her face, with a soiled diaper and a rash. I was furious at my mother's neglect. Somehow, I judged it worse when the neglect harmed my daughter than when it had harmed me. My mother wasn't allowed to be alone with my daughter again for a year and a half.

One evening, when Mother was in her sixties, she went out for dinner with a friend of hers. He noticed something on her face and went to brush it off her cheek. It didn't brush off, and he asked what it was. She touched her face and said, "One of the cats pooped on my bed last night, and I rolled over on it." She wasn't at all upset to realize it was still there.

Mother's friend and my husband Kevin worked in the same field. They had dinner together at a professional event shortly after this incident. The friend shared this story because of his alarm over my mother's attitude. To not be upset the cat pooped on the bed? To not take a hot shower with a wire scrub brush and disinfectant when you got cat shit on your *face*? Is this behavior *normal*?

No. Of course it isn't.

Grandma Jean obsessed over her own shit, starting early in her illness. She insisted someone else check to make sure her bowel movements looked "normal," whatever that meant. She took three tablespoons of mineral oil every day to make sure she went to the bathroom every morning, on schedule. She used a wind-up clock and set it every day to make sure she both took her mineral oil and moved her bowels at the same time every day. She started using the wind-up clock after the great northeast blackout of 1965, so she would know the correct time even in the event of another power failure. In later years, she had her keeper empty the toilet bowl by scooping the water into a bucket before Jean used the toilet so the water wouldn't obstruct the view of the contents.

Grandpa Bob had had the responsibility of checking Grandma's shit at first, but passed it down to Mary. At some point, Mary refused to continue doing it, and passed it down to Anita, who had no one to pass it down to. By age thirteen, one of my mother's chores was to check the contents of the toilet bowl after her mother went to the bathroom and reassure her everything was fine. Imagine being thirteen years old and having to look at your mother's bowel movements every day.

Small wonder my mother developed a problem with shit.

SEX

My information about my parents' marriage and sex life comes mostly from my father. Under normal circumstances, there would be no reason for a father to discuss with his daughter the intimate details of his marriage to his ex-wife, her mother. However, the lasting bitterness of their divorce and its effect on my life made the circumstances anything but normal. My stepmother Molly, to whom my father remained married for fifty-four years, was the other woman in my parents' divorce, so sex took center stage in explaining why the extramarital affair and subsequent divorce had happened.

Each member of my family had a different perspective on who did what to whom—who was guilty, who was innocent, and who was complicit. Even as my father lay on his deathbed, my sister-in-law brought up all the arguments and complaints of the decades-old family gossip. I was appalled. Two of the three people involved were dead. The third lay unconscious on the bed between us, dying. My family might lay the people to rest, but would never lay the topic to rest.

As I grew up, and especially as I learned how to be married

myself, I learned to ask the right questions of the right people to get what I think is the whole story, or at least most of it. My father, to his credit, never flinched from answering honestly, even when the answers cast him in a less than favorable light. After all, soft pedal it however one might, my father cheated on my mother and broke up his family. However, I can see the imprint of the legacy of Grandma Jean's illness and The French Court in the story. The surprise is not that my father left, but that he was ever there in the first place.

Hank and Anita were virgins when they married in 1955, as would have been expected at that time. As Hank put it, quoting a family friend, "Sex in a marriage is like plumbing in a house. When it's working, it's maybe 10%. When it's not working, it's 90%." Although Hank and Anita clearly got the mechanics right, or my brother and I wouldn't be here, there was something lacking that made sex closer to the 90% mark in their marriage, at least as far as Hank was concerned. Hank was dissatisfied enough with sex to question his own sexuality. He wasn't attracted to men, but assumed if he wasn't enjoying sex, there must be something wrong with him. Anita taunted him with his expressed concerns in the waning days of their marriage. For her part, Anita thought Hank was a sex fiend, like all men, because whenever she would show any physical affection or interest he would ask if she wanted to "fuck." That crudeness would make her immediately lose interest, which was of course his fault, not hers. At one point, Anita's menstrual period was late. As they counted back, Hank realized they had not had sex since before the previous period. It relieved the pregnancy worry, but demonstrated how infrequently they were intimate.

Anita had passive-aggressive tendencies. She was the least powerful person in her household growing up, as evidenced by the fact she performed Grandma's rituals rather than refuse as her father and sister had done. Since she couldn't rebel actively, she found passive ways to show her displeasure. Anita disliked confrontation and would find other means to get her way. One of the clearest examples of this behavior comes from her own youth.

Anita had a small shelf over her bed on which she kept trinkets. At some point when she was in high school, the shelf was cluttered. Her mother told her that if it wasn't clean when she went to school the next day, everything on the shelf would be thrown away. Anita forgot to clean the shelf that evening and was upset the next morning when she realized her belongings would be gone by the time she got home from school. She owned a small rubber mouse that looked real. Her mother was afraid of mice and had ordered the toy hidden from her sight. Anita placed the mouse on her shelf, knowing her mother would not touch the shelf with the mouse there. The passive manipulation worked, and Anita straightened the shelf when she got home.

Anita would listen politely when Hank offered criticisms or suggestions, nod her head in agreement, sometimes state she would do exactly what was being discussed, but not follow through. Anita's passive-aggressive avoidance of confrontation also meant never arguing with Hank. On at least two occasions during their marriage, Anita became angry about something Hank said and reacted by striking out at objects rather than talking to him about what was bothering her.

Anita's poor habits in cleanliness extended to her personal hygiene. Hank found himself increasingly turned off by the thought of touching her, knowing she had not bathed that day, and not knowing when, in fact, she had bathed last. Her hygiene became a constant source of argument between them. For example, at bedtime Hank would notice Anita's feet were black on the bottom. He would tell her she needed to clean her feet before she got into bed. She would get angry because he was treating her like a child and say that if he hadn't said anything, then of course she would have cleaned her feet before going to bed. So, the next time he noticed her feet were dirty, he wouldn't say anything until she got into bed. Then he would point out that she was in bed with filthy feet. Another argument would ensue. The arguments were not simply about the dirty feet, but also about Anita's lack of respect for Hank's feelings on the matter. There seemed no way for Hank to win.

Molly was Hank's secretary. Her own marriage was unhappy and breaking up for reasons unrelated to Hank. When two unhappy people work together, they easily form a bond. In this case, they eventually ended up in bed. For Hank, it was like discovering a whole new world. He recognized if he wasn't enjoying sex with Anita, it wasn't due to any lack on his part.

Realizing the torment Anita had put him through sexually, especially coupled with his growing distaste for the way she maintained the house, the children, and herself, Hank could find little reason for staying married. Anita, faced with an unfaithful husband, told him to move out and called his parents to tell them what their son had done. Relieved of having to make the decision of whether or not to move out, and of the arduous task of informing his parents, Hank moved out of Anita's house and in with the newly single Molly.

Grandma Jean was furious with Hank, but not surprised. He was a man, and acting as all men did. She had some satisfaction in getting her daughter and grandchildren back to New York City from Albany. Hank's mother, my Grandma Toby, later blamed Grandma Jean for the divorce because she believed Grandma Jean wanted the divorce and pushed Anita to go through with it. Hank would not have stayed married to Anita in any case, but obviously Grandma Jean was vocal at the time about wanting Hank out of Anita's life. I suspect Grandma Jean wanted Anita back under her control, which did not fully happen, but that would be another chapter in the story.

THE ETERNAL TRIANGLE

My parents, Anita and Hank, were married for six years. I was born on their third anniversary. One of the terms of their divorce agreement was that neither parent would tell the children the causes for the divorce until we were eighteen. That restriction didn't affect anyone else in the family.

I learned most of the story when I was thirteen from Aunt Mary and both my grandmothers; that was the age at which I first tried to get answers about all the undercurrents in my life I didn't understand. The tale was confusing when I first heard it. It only became more confusing as I grew older until I learned to ask questions of the principals: my mother Anita, my father Hank, and my stepmother Molly. Of the three, Molly was the most reluctant to discuss the events surrounding her own divorce as well as my parents'. I'm not sure even now that I know the whole truth, but I suspect no single person knows all of the story. The various members of my family have decided individually which parts they believe and which parts they disregard. Having gone through every part of the story during my many years of therapy, I've evolved a more balanced view. I realize everyone told their own truth. I've come to recognize how all sides might be true at the same time.

As an illustration of this middle road, I mention in another essay that "Hank was dissatisfied enough with sex to question his own sexuality ... Anita taunted him with his expressed concerns in the waning days of their marriage." From Anita, I learned Hank had confided he wondered if he might be gay. From Hank, I learned he had expressed that concern because he wasn't enjoying sex with Anita, and that she had thrown it back at him when they were divorcing. Since both sides acknowledge Hank had made the statement, I find it reasonable to conclude Anita would bring it up during an argument over sexuality in the context of divorce. By combining the stories, and knowing the storytellers well, I can honor both perspectives by stating what seems to be the objective truth.

No one's behavior was above reproach. Everyone was responsible, and no one was solely a victim. There was plenty of blame to go around. Anita never accepted that Hank was unhappy with their marriage and blamed Molly for having an affair with a happily married man. Molly never blamed anyone and never tried to excuse her own behavior. Grandma Toby blamed Grandma Jean. Grandma Jean blamed Hank. Hank blamed himself. The biggest regret of his life was that he hadn't ended the marriage when he knew he was unhappy, instead of waiting until he had fallen in love with someone else.

According to Anita, she and Molly were good friends. According to Molly, they were not. All agree that Molly and her husband attended the celebration of Anita and Hank's last anniversary together. I suspect Molly and her husband were work friends of Hank and Anita, but not necessarily close as a foursome. However, Molly was Hank's secretary. When Anita started to suspect there was another woman in Hank's life, she called Molly to see if she could get any information about who it was. Anita was presuming on a friendship that didn't really exist;

the two women didn't do anything together as friends without their husbands. Molly, of course, didn't know how to answer those questions, even though she knew everything that was going on. She was understandably evasive in her responses and probably lied to protect herself and Hank, which gave Anita even more reason to hate her when the truth came out.

Anita was furious at this betrayal from her perceived friend. She believed Molly had seduced a married man, and if it weren't for her, Anita and Hank would have lived happily ever after. When Dad and Molly came to pick us up for visits, Molly had to wait in the car. As a child, I didn't know why my mother hated Molly so much. I didn't understand Grandma Jean's venom whenever Molly's name came up; she nearly always spat on the ground after saying her name.

I knew Molly was my stepmother, and in the tradition of the fairy tales I loved, she must therefore be evil and wicked. From the things my family said, I gathered I was supposed to hate her. I felt guilty that I didn't hate her. I didn't fully love her until I was free of my mother and her influence on my relationships, but even as a child, I could appreciate that Molly was a caring stepmother.

Kevin and I had a courthouse wedding. My mother, his mother and sisters, and two dear friends were the only people in attendance. Part of our decision making was avoiding the brewing feud over which parents would be invited to attend. When Kevin and I joined the Catholic Church about four years later, we opted to have a small church wedding to solemnize our sacramental marriage. My mother refused to attend because Hank and Molly would both be there. A year and a half later, when Rebecca was baptized, all three of my parents were in attendance. It was the first time all three of them were in the same room at the same time in over twenty-two years. My mother tried to make it about herself, telling me during the service she was only there because she loved me. By then, I had learned to ignore her occasional martyrdom.

Anita would always start her story about the divorce with "I don't hold a grudge, but ...." The first time my mother-in-law heard the story was nearly twenty years after the fact. Viola and I had driven from Raleigh to Greenville for a day trip to visit my mother, and somehow the story came up. As we got back into the car to go home, Vi asked me how long ago the divorce had taken place. When I told her, she started to laugh. Anita's telling had held so much vitriol Vi had assumed it was of recent vintage.

My father paid my mother alimony for the rest of her life—over fifty-five years after a six-year marriage. In the early years, as Hank's career was developing and he was caring for five children, the alimony and child support payments were burdensome. Over time, especially after child support ended, $138 a month in alimony was an annoyance more than anything else. I regularly advised my father to stop paying, especially when I learned during my own divorce that the rule of thumb was that alimony or separate maintenance was paid for the same length of time as the marriage had lasted. Hank decided it would not be worth the aggravation of dealing with Anita if he stopped paying. I think it was a point of honor for him to continue paying; he was paying off his guilt.

Despite all the trauma involved with the end of Anita and Hank's marriage, and the viciousness of the ongoing interactions, the marriage between Hank and Molly was a love story for the ages. They weren't a demonstrative couple. I'm not sure I ever heard them say "I love you" other than when Hank would try to defuse an impending argument by saying "I love you, too, Pussycat!" They didn't hold hands or kiss. Neither of them was brought up to share private feelings where others could witness it. However, they took care of each other in ways large and small throughout fifty-four years of marriage.

Molly was a pillar of strength for Hank when he was suffering with a skull/spinal cord deformation that caused a major disruption in his life. The search for a diagnosis took months, and the recovery from surgery took even longer. Hank similarly supported Molly when she went through two surgeries for spinal stenosis several years apart. He was willing to sacrifice his own life by being her caregiver when she developed Parkinson's Disease, even though he was over eighty by then. During a visit, I asked him if he realized he was shortening his own life by caring for her. He told me he knew exactly what he was doing, and it was his choice. Molly refused to move to any kind of facility. He was going to honor her wishes as long as he could, even if it killed him.

A few months later, the rest of the family insisted on moving the couple to my brother's home in Oregon, far away from their extended family and friends in Maryland. Moving away was my father's second biggest regret in life. Molly died about nine months after the move, leaving Hank isolated except for one nuclear family, with no nearby friends. Hank knew they both would likely have died sooner had they remained in Maryland, but they would both have been surrounded by the people they loved and who loved them until the end. After Molly was buried in Oregon, there was no way Hank could consider leaving.

Together, Hank and Molly had an active social life and numerous friends. Hank had close relationships with many of the cousins he had grown up with in Brooklyn. He knew a wide variety of his cousins, from first to fifth cousins, on both sides. Molly was the eldest of five children, and the couple was close to all her siblings, niblings, and extended family. Molly's datebook, replaced every year or so, was filled with the names, birthdays, and anniversaries of all family members from both sides of their family and all their friends. When Molly died in 2016, family members lamented the loss of her datebook and all its information. A few years later, I happened to mention it to Dad, who produced their birthday book, which held almost all the same information. I quickly snapped photos of every page and transferred the information into a new datebook. It reminds me of how organized Molly was, as well as how many people loved her and Hank.

Hank and Molly did not have a perfect life, nor a perfect marriage, but they were happy together for fifty-four years. Hank was devastated by her death. Soon after, he learned he also had Parkinson's. He went through his decline without her, and missed her every day of the rest of his life, living about six and a half years as a widower.

During his final illness, every new person who entered his room at the hospital and rehab center had to read the poem he had written to her. It was in a golden frame beside her picture, which he spoke to every night. I can think of no better tribute to their love than to share his untitled poem here:

Have we neglected to renew our love,
to express feelings time has made habit?
Have the needs of living life so encompassed us,
we no longer hear our own hearts?
We are as two trees growing side by side,
with roots so intertwined
that they are separate but inseparable.
Your heart beats in my chest
Your pain cries out upon my lips
When I look at the world, I see it through your eyes.
No matter if the beauty of the skin fades
as we pass beyond our springtime.
My mind holds you constant,
My love unashamed and enduring.
Let us again open ourselves to each other,
to remember the joys and pains of shared feelings,
the special meaning of a touch, of eyes meeting.
Let us face ourselves, together.

MY FATHER

y parents divorced when I was three years old and
my brother Michael was a year and a half. He and I
lived with our mother. Therefore, I did not know
my father very well when I was young. It was the sixties. I was
the only child in my class who had divorced parents. All my
classmates had two parents at home. It was difficult to explain to
my friends why I did not have a father at home because I did not
understand it myself.

We lived in New York, in Queens, until I was ten. My father's
parents lived in Brooklyn, where my father had grown up. My
father and my stepmother, who lived close to Washington D. C.,
drove to Brooklyn one weekend each month. They would arrive
Friday evening and stay at my grandparents' home.

The following morning my father would come to pick us up.
Brooklyn was not far from Queens, but it was an hour-long ride.
We spoke about what had happened during the previous month.
We sang together, especially the drinking songs from my father's
high school days. *Beer! Beer! For Fort Hamilton!*

The kitchen always smelled delicious at my grandparents'
home. Grandma Toby was a typical Jewish mother. When she

knew her son and grandchildren were coming, she prepared all her best recipes. She served us lox and bagels because she knew that it was my favorite. She always made chopped liver, a favorite of my father's, a fruit salad or perhaps a cantaloupe, some chicken soup, roast chicken, vegetables, and always bread.

My grandmother's kitchen was kosher, meaning she observed Jewish dietary laws. She never served meat and milk together. We could not drink any milk with supper nor was there ever butter for the bread. We also had to wait for an hour after the meal if we wanted ice cream for dessert.

In the afternoon, my father and my grandfather often took my brother and me to a nearby park or playground. They pushed us on the swings, or caught us at the bottom of the slide. I thought the arms of my grandfather and my father were the strongest in the world. I felt safe when I was in them.

Our Saturdays together always ended much too soon. I wanted to stay longer at my grandparents' house. When we returned to our house, my brother and I were always sleepy.

My teen years were difficult. I didn't want to spend Saturdays with my parents or my grandparents. I wanted to go out and have fun with my friends. I was too busy to spend my time with old folks.

Once I got married, I learned how important family was. I got to know my father better. We developed a strong relationship as adults. He became a friend and advisor as much as a father. He was the first person I called when the pregnancy test was positive, at 6:45 in the morning. For my twenty-fifth birthday, I gave Dad a gold pocket-watch inscribed "For 25 years of Love." He proudly wore it for every formal event thereafter.[1]

We were very close during the last years of his life, when he was a lonely widower, quickly declining from Parkinson's disease. I gave him as much support and love as I could, and

---

1. I gave my mother a gold locket, similarly inscribed.

always looked for ways to make his life bearable. For his 90th birthday celebration, his closest friend and I put together a birthday party that included a room full of people singing to him, a family member playing the piano to entertain the guests, and a group video call with distant loved ones. My father felt loved and celebrated, which was probably the greatest gift I could have given him.

My grandparents and parents are gone. The days in which I felt myself secure in the arms of my father disappeared many years ago. I watched my daughter's close relationship with her father as she grew up and felt proud of them for building something my childhood had not had.

Sometimes, though, I long for the days when my father could swing me and catch me in his arms.

MY FATHER'S DAUGHTER

In 1988, I wrote a song for my father. Here are the lyrics.

My Father's Daughter

Verse 1

I never really knew you when I was just a child.
By the time I got to high school, I was obstinate and wild.
But now that I'm a parent and hold a tiny hand,
As I try to guide my young one, I think I understand.

Verse 2

The advice you tried to give me that I didn't want to take.
The pain you tried to save me, from mistakes I had to make.
The love that kept me near you, no matter where I went.
If I can be the parent you are, my life will be well-spent.

Chorus

And I want to say I love you. And I want to thank you, too,
For being an example of the things that I could do.
You have always been there for me, in good times and in bad.
My life has been made richer, 'cause I had you for my dad.

Verse 3

I dream of fame and fortune, to be worthy of men's praise.
But I'll never be a failure, though I follow humbler ways.
For I have known your wisdom, and I have felt your love.
To be my father's daughter is accomplishment enough.

Chorus

And I want to say I love you. And I want to thank you, too,
For being an example of the things that I could do.
You have always been there for me, in good times and in bad.
My life has been made richer, 'cause I had you for my dad.

THE COMB

A plastic comb is one of my most treasured possessions. I was visiting my parents—dad and stepmom—for two weeks between jobs. Mom had been diagnosed with Parkinson's Disease around four years earlier. Dad was her caregiver, but he was frightened by the changes he was seeing in her. He thought he could keep reminding her of the things she forgot. He would become angry that she couldn't remember. She would get frustrated and upset with his badgering.

While I was visiting, she had me help her open a package of three combs. She insisted on giving me one of them. I didn't want or need a comb, but I was pretty sure her gift was a token of affection, so I thanked her.

The next morning, I could hear Dad haranguing Mom. "Molly, where's the other one? There were three. Here's one on the counter, and there's one still in the package. Where's the third?" Mom's voice was becoming more petulant, though I couldn't hear her words. Dad seemed to think he could bully Mom into remembering.

I hurried through my bathroom routine and walked out combing my hair with the new comb. I went to where they were fussing and said something like "I really like this new comb you gave me, Mom." I gave her a kiss of thanks. Dad, of course, realized I had the missing comb. No apology to Mom, but at least the bullying stopped.

Mom passed about a year later. Sometime after, Dad was diagnosed with Parkinson's Disease. Last month, Parkinson's Dementia was added to the diagnosis. He is not nearly so cognitively affected as Mom was (yet).

That comb reminds me to treat Dad with the kindness he couldn't muster for Mom. That Dad isn't forgetting things because he doesn't want to remember. That no matter what he says or does, he doesn't mean any harm toward me or anyone else. He's doing the best he can with what he has. If he isn't meeting me halfway, it's because he can't. I have to reach out more than halfway to connect.

I will treat my Dad with all the love he showed me, as well as the respect and dignity anyone deserves. The comb reminds me of how his fear treated Mom and to avoid ever doing that to him. Or anyone else.

MY MOTHER

My mother was a talented woman. She was a published poet, a versatile actress, and an artist in both two-dimensional and three-dimensional media. She enjoyed knitting and frequently made clothing for people she loved. While I was in the hospital giving birth to her first grandchild, Mother sat in the lobby, knitting a sweater for the new baby, while chatting with my mother-in-law. After Rebecca had made an appearance, I sent one of our childbirth coaches to the lobby to find both grandmothers. I gave her one of the booties my mother had knitted to hold up so that Mother would recognize it. As it turned out, the bootie wasn't needed; the coach immediately saw my mother sitting in the waiting area, knitting, and went to her to announce that she was a grandmother.

Like most of the women in our family, Mother was short: four feet, ten inches. She was also disproportionately busty. I remember a Saturday evening in the 1970s when we were flipping through the two channels our television could receive. We happened to stop at a broadcast of The Porter Wagoner Show, where we saw a female singer. My mother took one look at the unknown singer, who would later emerge as a superstar named Dolly Parton, and exclaimed, "That woman is built like me!" Mother was fascinated by Dolly's rise to fame because she'd always considered her own body a liability.

In one of Mother's theater groups in Queens in the 1960s, she lost a role to another actress who was a couple of inches taller and several inches less busty. That actress was Estelle Getty, best known for *The Golden Girls*. The two women looked enough alike that someone in the group, seeing Estelle in a grocery store, asked her, "Are you her? Or are you the other one?" To which Estelle replied, "I'm her. The other one doesn't live around here." Mother loved telling that story, even before Estelle became famous. To me, it reflects how talented an actress my mother was. She lost a role to Estelle Getty not because of her acting, but because of her height.

My mother was a kindergarten teacher in Harlem when we lived in Queens. I think she chose those students because she believed she could make a difference. Later, she taught university classes in elementary education to undergraduate and master's level students in North Carolina. Making a difference in the lives of children became my own motivation for teaching. I chose special education instead of elementary education because whenever I worked in my mother's classroom, I was drawn to the children who were a little different or needed a little more help in order to succeed. Mother and I shared a love of working with young children and a philosophy that would eventually be encapsulated in the term "developmentally appropriate practice."

Mother was a volunteer. She believed in giving back to her community. Among other things, she served on the board of directors for the local crisis intervention hotline. She also made regular recordings of herself reading the newspaper. Her recordings were then condensed and distributed to bring the news to visually impaired people who couldn't read it themselves. Ironically, Mother developed macular degeneration late in life, becoming a member of the group she had previously volunteered to serve.

When we left New York for North Carolina, we discovered an absence of Chinese restaurants. That situation was unacceptable to a Jewish woman raised in Brooklyn. Mother set about learning how to cook Chinese food. I inherited Mother's willingness to experiment with cooking. When I lived in China, I had the opposite problem; I couldn't find the foods I had grown up with. I didn't learn much Chinese cooking because in China, Chinese food is just food. Instead, I learned how to make bagels and Italian sausage, things I craved but couldn't buy. I wasn't afraid to try new things in the kitchen because I'd witnessed Mother's adventurous spirit.

That adventurous spirit led her to take numerous cruises after her retirement to every part of the world except East Asia. I was sad that she never got to China or Japan, considering that she had studied both languages. We shared a fascination with other cultures, but had very different ways of experiencing them. Whereas Mother enjoyed sight-seeing and sampling local culture, I preferred to be immersed in a culture. Mother took cruises; I studied in Italy and taught in China.

Mother was fiercely independent. I think that was an evolving characteristic from the time she got divorced. She refused to be dependent on anyone, for anything. She disliked having someone tell her what to do. She did things the way she wanted to, regardless of what society said and inspired younger women to take control of their own destinies at a time when there were few role models.

Her independent attitude became problematic when she grew older. She would not inform us when something was wrong medically. Most often, we learned about things after the initial crisis had passed, such as when she was in an auto accident and broke bones in her hand, requiring surgery to set them, or when she had a heart attack and had to have a stent inserted. We learned about the injury that led to her death—falling and breaking her upper arm near the shoulder at age eighty-five— only because my daughter happened to call her. Mother declined quickly, dying three months after her fall.

My mother was a witty person. Her children and grandchildren all inherited her talent for repartee and sarcasm. One of my favorite memories centers around a joke that we continued to tell for over forty years. It started when I was around seven, and Mother was teaching me knock-knock jokes. One of them was

Knock, knock!

Who's there?

Anita

Anita who?

Anita go to the bathroom.

My mother's name was Anita, so I found this especially hilarious. I told the joke back to her.

Knock, Knock!

Who's there?

Anita

Anita who?

Anita gotta go to the bathroom.

Mother said, "No, it's 'Anita go to the bathroom.'" Smart ass that I was, even at that age, I answered, "Then go!"

The first time I told the joke that way, it was a true mistake. However, I continued to tell the joke that way every single time. And every single time, Mother fed me the set-up: "No, it's Anita go to the bathroom." Then I brought the joke home: "Then go!"

Well over forty years later, sitting in her kitchen, I told the wrong version of the joke again. She fed me the set-up, and I answered with the punchline. She stopped, looked at me, and said, "You always mess up that joke."

"That's because I know you'll always feed me the set-up."

Even as I'm writing this, I have tears in my eyes remembering the look of dawning realization on her face and the laughter that we shared.

Shared laughter is a blessing. So was my mother.

THE APPLE OF HER EYE

I was the apple of Grandma Jean's eye. I was the oldest grandchild and, for seven years, the only girl. Sometimes she and Grandpa Bob would pick me up from our apartment in Flushing and take me to their apartment in Brooklyn, where I would spend the night. This was a special treat I was given, one never offered to my brother nor to my male cousins.

My memories of visits to Grandma and Grandpa's apartment are jumbled together. I think that's because there were so many of them. I remember taking walks with Grandpa Bob and getting ice cream cones. I remember going to watch parades virtually around the corner from their apartment. Grandma Jean would sing songs with me and teach me little dances. I would sit on Grandpa's lap and watch Jackie Gleason on Saturday night. At bedtime, I got a mug of warm milk with a pat of butter and a little bit of sugar in it. I had a collection of toys at their apartment that none of the other grandchildren ever played with. None of them were ever allowed to visit because they were boys. Grandma Jean didn't allow boys to visit.

Grandpa Bob would make me dinner, which he and I would

eat together. The only problems were when the meal occasionally included cooked carrots. I hated cooked carrots and would refuse to eat them; I know now that the problem was the texture of the cooked carrots. Grandma Jean would stand and watch us, rocking back and forth with her gloved hands behind her back. She would try to make Grandpa make me eat the carrots. I would spit them out. Poor Grandpa was stuck between two strong-willed females. I don't remember ever eating those carrots, though I was threatened with dire consequences if I didn't. The carrots never did show up at breakfast, either, in spite of the threats to the contrary.

I never saw Grandma Jean eat. After Grandpa and I ate, I would be sent into the living room to play with my toys while Grandpa fed Grandma Jean. I was not allowed to enter the kitchen while Grandpa was preparing Grandma Jean's dinner and feeding her. I remember standing outside the door and whining because it was taking too long. That was the only thing I ever did that was guaranteed to get me scolded.

Even when I wasn't visiting Grandma Jean and Grandpa Bob, they would take me out for ice cream or to the coffee shop or just for rides in the car. On rare occasions, one of the boys might be allowed to come along, but usually it was just me. I remember Grandma Jean shopping to buy me a doll, and then being annoyed because I insisted she buy the boy doll for one of the boys in the family. I knew I was special because Grandma Jean told me so all the time in many ways. I was a girl.

When Aunt Mary's third child, my cousin Abigail, was born when I was almost seven, Grandma Jean was thrilled to have another granddaughter, and I was replaced. Of course, Abby couldn't start spending the night or even start learning all the little songs right away. At some point between Abby's birth and our move to North Carolina when I was ten, Grandma and Grandpa moved to Queens to be closer to their children and grandchildren. By the time we left, Abby was the new apple of Grandma Jean's eye. Even though I was a little jealous at being replaced, I was glad Grandma Jean had Abby. Otherwise, she might have missed me too much.

CAR DREAMS

hen I was seven years old, I woke up from a nightmare I knew I had had before. That is the first time I remember having the recurring nightmare I call the "car dream." Obviously, I had had the dream even before I was seven. I have continued to have the same dream in some variation throughout my life, especially in periods of stress.

In the dream, I am in the back seat of a car. My mother is in the driver's seat, and Michael, my younger brother, is in the front passenger seat. Using car seats or having children sit in the back weren't safety concerns in the 1960s. Mother parks the car, gets out, and goes into a building. Somehow the car starts to roll forward, and the engine starts. Michael is too young and too little to steer the car, so it is up to me to get into the front seat and get control of the runaway car. I try to get into the front seat, but I can't climb over the seat. I try to grab the steering wheel from the back seat, but I can't reach because my arms are too short. I can't see over the driver's seat to avoid obstacles. No matter what I do, I can't control the car.

Because of the car dream, I was terrified of learning to drive. I was the youngest member of my high school class. When everyone else was taking the practical portion of the driver's education class, I was still too young to get my learner's permit. By the time I was old enough to take the driving course, I was too afraid to get behind the wheel of a car. I didn't get my driver's license until I was twenty-one. Even then, I only got it because I had to.

As a driver, I was prone to panic attacks when I was lost or in a new place. I would drive white-knuckled through streets I didn't recognize, screaming at the top of my lungs. I didn't dare stop the car, because I knew instinctively I would never get back into the car if I got out. Once I figured out where I needed to go, other drivers were very polite about letting me into traffic so I could get there. They seemed to recognize that a crazy lady was driving my car.

Only once was I so hopelessly panicked I had to park the car and get out. I was in one of the least savory parts of Raleigh on a Saturday afternoon when it happened. I saw a phone booth, so I pulled the car over to call Kevin for help. I locked the car and walked trembling over to the phone. I must have looked terrible. A man with ragged clothing sitting in a doorway came to my rescue. He showed me how to make a phone call from a pay phone without any change. Then he stayed with me, talking about the weather, sports, anything, until Kevin arrived and took me home. The car stayed where it was until the next day.

When I was thirty, I finally realized my dreams had nothing whatsoever to do with driving; they were about responsibility. Even before I was seven years old, I knew at some level that my mother was not taking appropriate care of Michael and me. Since I was older, it was my job to protect him. While I may not have liked Michael, I accepted him as my responsibility. However, it was a responsibility I wasn't up to.

I couldn't control the car that was our lives.

CHILDHOOD NEGLECT

When Catholics recite the Act of Contrition, they ask for forgiveness both for sins of commission and sins of omission, "for what I have done and what I have failed to do." My mother didn't commit many sins against Michael and me as we were growing up; she wasn't a particularly abusive parent. She did, however, fail to do many things as a parent. Mother's usual approach to a task she didn't want to do was to ignore it until it went away, someone else did it, or it absolutely had to be done. Unfortunately, that strategy is not very effective when dealing with children.

My mother was so neglectful that in the 1990s I confronted my father and asked him why he never took her to court to try to get custody of us. He knew most of what had gone on in our home, although he hadn't known the full extent of it. He had tears in his eyes from the things he had just learned about my childhood that he had never heard before. He said that in the 1960s, in order for a father to gain custody of his children against the wishes of the mother, he would virtually have had to prove she was a prostitute who was turning tricks in front of the children. Back then, even social service agencies weren't likely to investigate children who were unclean or unhealthy. Teachers now have a legal mandate to report even suspected neglect or abuse to the appropriate agency, but in the 1960s, no such requirement existed.

When I was in the third grade and had a toothache, there was no school social worker around to find out I had never seen a dentist in my life. There was no one to follow up and find out that one of my teeth had rotted in my mouth because I never brushed my teeth. The dentist who pulled my tooth also found eleven cavities. That's eleven cavities in the mouth of an eight-year-old, plus one rotten tooth. I never brushed my teeth because no one ever told me to. No one expected me to. My class had had lessons on brushing teeth, complete with an oversized molar and a giant toothbrush, but without follow-up at home, the lessons meant nothing. My mother never brushed her teeth. She had all thirty-two of her teeth with no fillings until she was thirty-five.

While we lived in New York, Michael and I saw our father once a month. He and Molly lived near Washington, D. C. They would drive up on Friday after work and spend the night at his parents' apartment in Brooklyn. They would pick us up Saturday morning, and we would spend the day at Grandma Toby and Grandpa Irving's home, returning home Saturday evening.

Mother would make sure Michael and I took baths on Friday night before Dad came on Saturday. She had to make sure because it was not part of the daily routine to do so. I did not take a bath every night. I did not take a bath every other night. I did not take a bath once a week. I don't know how often I took baths. I took them as often as I was told. When I stayed with Dad and Molly during vacations and they made me take baths every day, I thought they were weird.

I did the same thing with changing underwear. I just changed it when I took a bath. It seemed wasteful to change it more often. That's what Mother did, so that's what I did. Looking back, it amazes me no one at school noticed; I had to be a stinky kid.

Michael had asthma. Dad was forever telling Mother to take Michael to get his allergy shots and to make sure Michael took his medicine. Mother absolutely would not take Michael to get his shots. She always lied to Dad and said she had. She made me lie, too. I never understood why Mother refused to take Michael for his shots regularly. I know she learned from Grandma Jean to distrust all doctors, but she never sought alternative therapies for Michael either. I think maybe she was being stubborn because it was Dad who was telling her she had to do something. She preferred to put her own son at risk rather than do something Dad told her to do.

Throughout their marriage, my father had told my mother he preferred modest women. He didn't like painted fingernails. He didn't like women who smoked. When he chose Molly, a woman with painted nails who smoked up until she and Dad married, my mother reacted by taking up smoking. She did it as a "fuck you" to my father, though it didn't affect him in the slightest. She remained a heavy smoker for the rest of her life until she had to be hospitalized and moved into a nonsmoking assisted living facility shortly before her death. My brother had developed asthma by three years old, but Mother smoked in the house and car anyway. I had frequent upper respiratory infections as a child and remain prone to developing bronchitis as an adult. My mother's "fuck you" hurt her children more than her ex-husband.

Sometimes Mother would give Michael his medicine, but then when it ran out, she wouldn't get it refilled. To be honest, she wasn't really good about giving him his medicine regularly either. Once when we spent the night at Aunt Mary's house, Mother dropped us off without Michael's medicines. Sure enough, Michael had an asthma attack, and Aunt Mary had to contact Mother to get the medicines.

I describe elsewhere Mother's approach to house training her dogs. Given what the floors of both our apartment in New York and our house in North Carolina were like, and the pervasive smell of both places, it would be hard to say our home was ever "clean." Yet from the time Mother started working after her divorce, when I was about four, until I started ninth grade at thirteen, we had a live-in housekeeper. Sally, the last housekeeper, was with us for seven years, moving when we moved from New York to North Carolina to be closer to her family in Virginia. She did general housekeeping, laundry, childcare, and cooked for Michael and me, but she refused to clean up after the animals. Even after Sally retired, we had someone coming in to clean once a week. My mother was perfectly able to reconcile the foul odor and the animal feces with having a housekeeper. In addition to ignoring tasks she didn't want to do, Mother was also a master at ignoring uncomfortable details.

Even trauma was best dealt with by ignoring it. When I was nine, a man followed me home from the candy store to our apartment building. He got onto the elevator with me and pressed the button for the third floor, while I pressed the button for the sixth floor, the highest floor in the building. He had his back to me, then turned around with his penis out of his pants. He wanted me to touch it. He put his hand under my skirt and into my panties, telling me I had a "cut" there. At least, that was the word I thought I heard, though he probably used a more vulgar word that in my innocence I didn't recognize. When the elevator stopped at the third floor, he pressed the button for the fourth. He kept trying to get me to touch him. At the fourth floor, he pressed the button for the fifth. I started to cry. He begged me not to cry, then got off the elevator at the fifth floor. I ran home when the elevator doors opened at the sixth floor.

My mother called the police. They came and questioned me. I was not coddled or comforted. I put on my pajamas and got into bed. As far as I was concerned, my day was over. Therapy? Not even a hint of it. Mother told me not to tell anyone about the incident, especially not my father. No one ever discussed it with me again, but my friends and I had our Barbies role playing variations of the "elevator man" for months, starring Ken as a pedophile.

I stayed home from school one Friday when I was thirteen, complaining of a strange stomach ache. When Dad and Molly came to pick us up for the weekend, I mentioned that over dinner. Molly pulled me aside and asked if it was my period. I told her I didn't know, since I'd never had one.

That Monday evening, I found a brown stain in my underwear, indicating my first period; Molly had been correct. My mother used tampons and wouldn't allow me to use them for my first period. She didn't have anything else in the house. She tore up an old bedsheet and folded it around a core of paper towels to fashion a diaper for me. I didn't know I could have asked in the school office for more appropriate supplies. Instead, I had to wear that diaper for the whole day until I got home, and my mother could give me supplies and explain how to use them.

I couldn't understand how my stepmother, who didn't live with me, had recognized my period was coming, but my mother hadn't. I knew I wasn't prepared for the practical aspects, but I didn't understand why my mother wasn't; I thought she should have already had supplies on hand. While this may seem less neglectful than some of my mother's other lapses, it remains a painful memory tinged with shame when I should have been celebrating starting womanhood.[1]

A couple of months later, I won a pet rabbit at an Easter giveaway. We knew that if Ottavio, our beagle, got hold of the rabbit, he would want to play with it. The problem was he might hurt it, since he tended to pick up things like kittens by their heads. Somehow, my mother couldn't manage to find time to buy a cage

---

1. Part of my own healing involved parenting my daughter as I wished I had been parented. After she started her period, I reserved a house at the beach for a weekend and invited other women and girls to stay there. We initiated Rebecca into womanhood with a period of confinement followed by a moonlight ritual on the beach.

for the rabbit, even though she knew the danger of keeping the rabbit in a cardboard box and knew the latch on my bedroom door wasn't secure. One week after the rabbit came home with me, Ottavio got into my room and killed my rabbit. I found the body. My mother dealt with it by taking me out to buy clothes to stop my crying. The dead rabbit was still in my bedroom when we got home.

At one point when I was fourteen, I needed shoes. By that age, my feet had pretty much stopped growing, so I finally had more than one pair of shoes at a time. Among the shoes I owned was a lovely pair of black velvet ballerina slippers my father and Molly had bought me, along with my first formal gown, as a birthday gift. After my school shoes wore out, I started to wear the other shoes in my closet, telling my mother I needed new shoes. I went through each old pair of shoes I had, reminding my mother each week that I desperately needed shoes. Finally, the only shoes I had left to wear were my beautiful black velvet slippers. They were shoes more suited to dancing than going to school, but I didn't have a choice. I had worn out everything else.

Mother took Michael and me and some of her college student friends to a nearby historic town to do some sightseeing. It was a snowy winter. As I walked across the snow, one of our friends noticed my shoes. He told me I was going to ruin my shoes wearing them in snow. I told him they were already ruined. He asked me why I was wearing them. I told him I didn't have any others. He asked me if I had told my mother. I said yes. He asked me why she hadn't taken me to get new shoes. I shrugged. I saw him talking with my mother a little while later. I don't know what he said to her, but that weekend I got new shoes. It was too late for my black velvet ballerina slippers.

Despite my awareness of my mother's neglect, I didn't do a good job of protecting my daughter from her. I was trying so hard to love and trust my mother that I overlooked the fact she wasn't trustworthy. The first time my mother neglected Rebecca was when she babysat for her in infancy. Rebecca soiled her diaper, but my mother didn't change her. Rebecca was always very uncomfortable with poop in her diaper and insisted on being changed. She ended up crying herself to sleep. When I arrived home to find my daughter sleeping with a dirty diaper, her face flushed and sweaty, I knew immediately what had happened. I refused to allow my mother to babysit again for a year and a half.

Rebecca played a unique role in my mother's life. Rebecca was the only person who could confront my mother over her hurtful behavior without being stonewalled. At three years old, Rebecca tearfully asked her grandmother to quit smoking. Mother treated the request respectfully, although she didn't change her behavior. Years later, as a young adult, Rebecca scolded my mother for not informing us she had been in an auto accident and needed surgery to repair her hand. Usually, Mother would react to such a scolding with deflection and stubborn refusals, but she always accepted that Rebecca had the right to question and correct her.

When Rebecca was eleven, she spent a couple of nights with my mother during a school break when Kevin and I had to work. Rebecca preferred visiting her grandmother to spending the week in a daycare setting. At the time, there was a nail in Mother's kitchen flooring that had popped up. Grandma Jean, by then living with Mother, kept pointing out that the nail was a hazard and told Mother to hammer it down. My mother always dug in her heels when someone told her what to do, so she pointedly ignored Grandma's nagging. Rebecca sliced the ball of her foot on the nail head. My mother responded by wiping it off with a damp paper towel. No running water. No soap. No antiseptic. My mother's pets used the floors as toilets. The nail had to have been filthy. When I picked up Rebecca the next day, I asked her how her foot was. She showed me her badly infected foot. We went straight to an urgent care center for treatment, which included a round of antibiotics and a tetanus shot.

When Rebecca was thirteen, my mother came to visit us in Tallahassee. Both of them begged for Rebecca to spend the night with her grandmother at her hotel. When Kevin and I arrived to pick them up and return them to our house at 1:00 the next afternoon, I learned my mother had not given Rebecca anything for breakfast. Mother had made coffee in the room, which was all she ever had for breakfast, but didn't wake up early enough to take Rebecca to the hotel's breakfast and didn't give her permission to go alone. I pulled Rebecca aside and apologized to her. I felt guilty for once again failing to protect my daughter from her neglectful grandmother.

There is only one way in which my mother was overtly abusive, her one "sin of commission." When she got tired of the arguing between Michael and me, she would spank us. Since she was short, she had small hands. She reasoned her hands couldn't hurt us enough; therefore, she used the leather dog leash to spank us, usually on our legs. She didn't whip us hard enough to break the skin, but the welts she left were painful. Perhaps in the 1960s that wouldn't have seemed unusual. I hope any parent using a leather strap to beat a child now would be placed under the supervision of child protective services.

Mother's use of the dog leash ended with an episode of particular empowerment for me. I was around twelve. There was some bickering going on between Michael and me, and we were sent to our rooms to await spanking. I decided I wasn't going to tolerate any more beating, so I looked around my room for something to hit back with. The only thing I could find was a wire hanger from the closet. I sat on the edge of my bed, holding the hanger in one hand, hitting it against the other palm, waiting. My mother walked in, holding the leash. My resolve must have shown in my face. She saw me sitting there, registering my posture, expression, and that hanger rhythmically hitting my palm, all in one glance. She gave me a lecture on my behavior and left my room. She never threatened me with the strap again.

Children who grow up in a neglectful household don't necessarily realize it's neglectful until they leave that environment. For me, it wasn't until I became a parent and realized the kinds of things a parent does for their child that I realized how poor a parent my mother had been. I was angry and told my therapist about the things my mother had not done that she should have done. My therapist wondered if perhaps my mother just didn't know any better. I shook my head, not knowing whether to laugh or cry. She asked what I was thinking. I told her my mother had been a kindergarten teacher and then a university professor of elementary education. It was impossible to believe she didn't know what young children needed.

THE QUEEN AND I

While we were living in New York, my mother was
involved with community theater. When we moved
to a small town in North Carolina, she got involved
with the drama department of the local university. Since she was
significantly older than the students—mostly Drama majors—but
not quite old enough to be their parent, she became a mother *in
absentia* for many of them. The circle of drama majors who
frequented our home tended to be among the most talented,
since they were the students who were cast in shows over and
over, along with my mother.[1]

After rehearsal, at 11:00 or later, they would come over to
play cards, relax, and wind down after the hard work of
rehearsal. Card playing would go on for three hours or more.
The drinking age at the time was eighteen for wine and beer, so
these occasions were liberally lubricated with alcohol. Being the
1970s, there was also plenty of cannabis. My mother did not

---

1. When Kevin and I were engaged, I joked that if the marriage lasted ten years, I
was going to write a book titled "The Queen and I." By using that title for this
chapter, I am making good on that promise.

permit the students to smoke weed in her house, but the river was two blocks away. If someone wanted to get high, they had only to ask, "Do you want to take a walk down to the river?" Everyone understood the code.

Even though I would go to sleep at a reasonable time for a twelve-year-old (and older as the years passed), some nights I would be awakened by the noise. The door to my bedroom was off the kitchen, which is where these gatherings took place. On the weekends, I would stay up to join in. If they needed a fourth for Spades, the card game of choice, I was it.

The conversation was probably typical for a group of talented, creative young people at around twenty years old: sex and drugs. Despite the age difference, I learned to fit right in. I had always been a smart ass; one of my mother's adult friends had called me that from the time I was nine years old. Even at that age, I was comfortable conversing with adults. When adults teased me, I teased right back. Spending time with these students who were closer to my age than to my mother's, but still a world apart, I learned the nuances of the double entendre. Being quick with a sarcastic comeback was a survival skill at our dinner table. There were many allusions I didn't catch, but I developed a vocabulary and a worldliness far beyond my years. I also learned that many of the young men I was spending my time with were gay. By the time I was thirteen, I knew exactly what that meant. In spades.

My mother had always been involved in the fine arts: theater, art, and poetry. She developed many close relationships with men who were gay, both men her own age and the younger college-aged friends she met through the university. I am aware of only one male companion who was also a sexual partner. Their relationship developed from her poetry group, even though he was twenty years her junior. Besides that one brief relationship, every man I watched her become close to was gay. She may well have been attracted to the same characteristics in gay men that later attracted me, since her upbringing was as traumatic as mine, if not more so. The gay men who were part of our lives tended to be kind, gentle men who were in touch with their own feelings and comfortable with the feelings of others. My impression, though, is that my mother felt safe with men who showed no sexual interest in her.

Maybe these talented gay men became my models for what a man should be. Or maybe, as one psychiatrist suggested to me, my childhood was so neglectful that I looked for nurturing men, and gay men were more overtly nurturing than straight men. Whatever the reason was, many of the boys I dated in high school ended up being bisexual or gay men as adults. Years later, one of my former boyfriends told me he and another old boyfriend of mine had hooked up in college and then talked about what my reaction would be if I had known. It was laughter, as it turned out.

When I was a freshman in college, I worked at a snack bar on campus. I invited one of my customers to meet me at a string quartet concert. When I showed up, he had two friends with him. One of them was Kevin. We saw each other two days later at one of the other snack bars on campus, started talking, and became inseparable friends thereafter. It was an entirely platonic relationship, since Kevin was a gay male, and I was a straight female.

Whenever Kevin talked about his dreams for the future, he always talked about his vision of a house with a white picket fence, a two-car garage, two point five children, and a dog in the yard. I asked him how he thought a gay man was going to be able to have those things, especially the kids part. Surrogate pregnancies and IVF weren't on the horizon in 1976. The gay rights movement was still in its infancy; same-sex marriage didn't yet exist as a concept. We couldn't talk about those options. Was he going to get married and then divorce his wife? He didn't know. Did he want to adopt? No. He knew what he wanted; he'd figure out how to get it later.

At the end of that school year, saddened by our impending separation, we found ourselves in bed together. We both enjoyed the experience, much to Kevin's surprise. With that barrier overcome, we had to reassess our relationship. Suddenly, we had to face the possibility of being more than friends. Even though Kevin went home for the summer, we saw each other every few weeks. We allowed the physical part of our relationship to develop. By the time school started again in the fall, we were a couple. Two years later, we married after Kevin's graduation.

The fact that we married did not mean Kevin was any less gay than when he was going to bars looking for male partners. It meant he loved me enough to choose a life of monogamy with a woman over a life of gay sex. Other people tried to tell Kevin he was by definition bisexual. He insisted that he was gay, and I was an aberration, albeit a pleasurable one.

In truth, I think Kevin falls at the far "gay" end of the gay/straight continuum. His sexuality was never a binary choice. He has whatever inborn traits make a man gay. His preferences and fantasies are all about males. The fact he was able to enjoy sex with me did not make him straight. All that happened was he fell in love with me, not my genitals, and loving me, he learned to make love to me as well.

I married Kevin because I loved him. I don't know why Kevin married me. I never understood it and never will. It's possible he was seeking a "beard," a woman to function as his disguise in the straight world. However, late in our marriage we met a man who was dating a male friend of ours. This man was married with children. His wife didn't know of her husband's sexual preference or infidelities. He boasted about "respecting" her by not having sex with anyone else in their home state, but only when he traveled for work. Kevin was disgusted by this man, who was using his wife as a beard. If that was the role I played in Kevin's life, I don't think it was intentional.

Perhaps Kevin thought I was the best chance he had at happiness in a world that offered him few choices. He may also have thought he was the best I could do, and therefore sought to rescue me from my unhappy home life. What a shame our choices seemed so limited when Kevin and I were only twenty-two and twenty respectively.

I've always wondered why Grandma Jean's legacy, the gift of The French Court, has been so pronounced in me as compared to the rest of my generation. My brother and cousins have their issues to be sure, but haven't struggled with mental illness to nearly the extent that I have. We should share a similar genetic inheritance from Grandma Jean. Michael and I also had similar environmental influences. Why, then, have I suffered the effects of mental illness so much more? In part, it's because I have an Autism Spectrum Disorder, a form of neurodivergence that is separate from mental illness, but it also springs from the consequences of choosing a gay husband.

I married my best friend because I loved him more than anyone in the world. I wasn't exactly sure why he married me, but it didn't matter; I was too happy to have him in my life to want to examine why. The marriage lasted twenty-nine years, and most of it was successful by any measure. Our home was warm and loving. Visitors described walking into our house as walking into a hug. We supported each other through joy and sorrow.

The one big problem was that every single day Kevin reminded me I lacked something he wanted: a penis. He looked at cute guys passing by, and I knew I could never compete because I wasn't a guy. I could've been the world's hottest girl, but I still wouldn't have had a penis. I learned to do things to please him sexually, but he still masturbated every day so he could have time to fantasize about the things he wished he was doing. He begged me to set up threesomes with the two of us and another man so he could have what he wanted without being unfaithful to me. When the Internet became available, he started downloading gay porn and leaving it visible on the family computer desktop where I could see it. Even our daughter was able to find his porn without looking for it, which ultimately lead to her learning the truth about her father's sexuality.

In that situation, I developed incredible stress. No matter how much Kevin loved me, he couldn't have loved me enough to undo the harm he was doing by constantly rejecting me as a woman. He thought my genitals looked like a wound; they even bled once a month. He could never have reassured me sufficiently he would not leave me because he wanted a man, which was, in the end, what he did. Perhaps I should have considered divorce as a better environment for my own mental health, but I remained deeply in love with Kevin until after we separated.

Most people would probably consider the marriage a success, even though ultimately it ended in divorce. It broke down because of Kevin's sexuality, but also because Kevin had a job that demanded 100% travel. He was frequently out of town from Sunday evening to Friday afternoon. I went to China for five months to teach English, hoping he would miss me, but a marriage requires care and feeding. By the time I returned, Kevin had decided he wanted to live his life openly as a gay man.

We were together for thirty-two years, married for twenty-nine, during which we were each other's best friends, enjoyed spending time together, and had an active and satisfying sex life. We have a lovely and talented daughter who, in spite of the legacy of mental illness that she inherited, is an incredibly gifted woman who knows she was a loved and cherished child. Maybe when Kevin and I married, it was because we recognized something in each other that was right, that transcended sexual preferences. Still, in the context of making good marital choices, ours has to be among the best examples of the worst decision making.

BETTER LIVING THROUGH
CHEMISTRY

My brother and I aren't close. We never were. When people ask if there was some particular event that drove us apart, I answer, in all seriousness, "He was born." I really never forgave him for that.

My mother tried to prepare me for the birth of my little brother. I was sixteen months old, so she expected me to revert from the cup to the bottle. When the new baby came home from the hospital, Mother offered me a bottle while she fed the baby. I was having none of that. I retreated into myself, big girl cup in hand. According to my mother, that was the beginning of a personality change that never reversed.[1]

I first heard that story when I was hospitalized with depression at age thirty-seven. I had been initially diagnosed at thirty. There was no particular crisis in my life at the time, so there didn't seem to be any need to try medication. Two years later, stress at work led me to ask for something to deal with anxiety. I

---

1. The same story may also represent the first signs of my autism. My mother said my personality changed from happy and affectionate to being stand-offish and refusing physical affection. That is consistent with what other parents report about their children with ASD at about the same age.

was so surprised at how well the anti-anxiety medication worked I asked the psychiatrist for antidepressants, just to see what would happen. He prescribed Prozac.

Prozac is supposed to take four to six weeks to take effect. I had taken Prozac for four days—*four little pills*—when I noticed the effect. Kevin was with me at work that day because my class was performing for the last day of school. The performance was a required part of a grant I had received. When the plans got upset due to outside circumstances, I lost my sound system. Fortunately, I had a little grant money left and was able to rent one on short notice. Both Kevin and my teaching assistant commented on how well I had dealt with the situation and solved the problem without getting upset. That behavior was not typical for me. When I reported the quick effect to my psychiatrist, he made a differential diagnosis of dysthymia, chronic low-level depression. In other words, I had never been normal in my life, probably since the birth of my little brother, if my mother's story is accurate.

Once my depression was cured, at least in a chemical sense, my view of the world changed. *Every*thing changed. It was as if until that time the whole world stood in a circle, hands joined, with their backs to me. They were involved in some intricate dance, the steps of which were written down in a manual. Everyone else had been given a copy of this manual at birth, but I hadn't gotten a copy. Most people just ignored me because I obviously couldn't follow the dance. A few kind people tried to teach me the dance before giving up in frustration because I was clumsy, stupid, or just plain hopeless. Some, but not too many after I finished high school, ridiculed or ostracized me because I couldn't do what everyone else did as naturally as breathing. Only a handful of people left the larger circle to dance with me the way I danced, regardless of the steps everyone else was doing. My husband. My best friend. Not many at all.

After the Prozac took effect, I could see the rest of the world didn't have a manual. There was no secret they knew that I didn't. They had learned how to dance from each other, each person adding their own variations to the dance, so it was ever changing and evolving. The circle wasn't closed to me at all. They had all dropped hands so they could reach out to me, and turned to face me with smiles of welcome on their faces. I had tears on my cheeks as I took my first tentative steps to join them.

The fact this all happened so quickly also meant my depression had a basis in brain chemistry. Was it hereditary? Probably, given my family history. I learned nearly thirty years later that not only was my brain chemically different from other people's, but it was wired differently. Specifically, I learned ten days before my fifty-ninth birthday that I have an Autism Spectrum Disorder. Even after getting on antidepressants, I still struggled to be "normal."

Would medication have helped Grandma Jean?

At some point in the 1990s, after again being diagnosed with OCD, Grandma was put on Paxil, another antidepressant. Her symptoms showed some improvement in that she was less anxious with the minor disruptions that interfered with her routines. However, she then used taking the medication as a new method to manipulate my mother. If Mother wasn't home at the correct time for Grandma's dose, Grandma wouldn't take it. She also wouldn't take it earlier or later than the scheduled time or with her keeper. She used the medication to control my mother even more. Mother decided the improvement wasn't worth the cost, and Grandma stopped taking the medication that had helped her.

LOOKING FOR GOD

Grandpa Bob was a kosher butcher. That means the meat he sold had been ritually slaughtered and prepared in keeping with Jewish dietary laws. However, Grandma Jean stopped keeping a kosher home immediately after her father's funeral. I mean that quite literally. When she walked through the door to their apartment after the funeral, she went straight to the kitchen and combined the dishes that had previously been kept separate for meat or dairy. She didn't explain her actions to anyone, so I don't know if she stopped believing in God and His laws because He had let her father die or if she had only been keeping kosher to please her father. Whatever Grandma Jean's rationale was, any vestige of religious practice in her home died along with Great-grandpa Morris.

My mother, who was eight when her grandfather died, had a secular upbringing, and raised Michael and me the same way. Mother was a very curious mix of traditions. She liked the secular aspect of holiday celebrations, but disliked anything that smacked of religion. We exchanged Christmas gifts in our home, but we weren't allowed to have a Christmas tree. The gifts were just piled on the floor on Christmas morning. My pile was bigger than Michael's because my birthday is December twenty-fifth. It was a pretty crappy way to celebrate either a birthday or a holiday.

We also celebrated Chanukah, complete with candle lighting and gift giving, but without any prayers. My mother had always shown her affection by giving gifts, mostly small tokens of affection that showed you were thought of rather than anything extravagant. Those holidays when gifts were given were especially fun for her when we were young. I think her affection for Christmas sprang from the opportunity it offered to give presents to others.

I knew I was Jewish, but I couldn't have told you what that meant. I knew the name Jesus; there was a picture of him on a wall at Dad and Molly's house. I knew I wasn't supposed to believe in him, but I didn't know why not, nor what it meant to believe in a person. I didn't really know what it meant to believe in God. I knew all about Greek and Roman gods, but they were ancient. I had no concept of religion or religious practice.

I remember one Sunday staring through my telescope out of my bedroom window from our sixth-floor apartment in Flushing to the people in the street below. They were all dressed up and walking into the church down the block. I had no idea what happened inside a church. I was a little scared to find out. I knew one of my best friends went to church. I had gone to a couple of church bazaars with her and bought some dresses. The people seemed nice. When I asked my mother why we didn't go to church, she said it was because we were Jewish. That wasn't an answer.

In fourth grade, I saw a display of pretty scenes at the candy store. When I had spending money for Christmas gifts, I bought a small one for my mother and a larger one for Dad and Molly. Mother was helping me wrap the gift for Dad. She asked me why I was giving it to them. I told her I thought it was pretty. She asked me if I knew what it was. I didn't. She asked me if my dad celebrated Christmas. I told her yes, he and Molly had a tree at their house. She then explained to me the pretty gift I'd bought was a nativity scene celebrating the story of Christmas, and it wouldn't be appropriate to give it to them if their household was Jewish. Since they celebrated Christmas, she allowed me to wrap it and give it to them. I confessed I had bought her a smaller one. I had to choose another gift for my mother.

After we moved to North Carolina, several things happened that gave me answers. During that first year, when I was in sixth grade, my mother's cousin's son had his bar mitzvah in nearby Virginia, and we attended. It was the first time I had ever been inside a synagogue, and I was impressed. I asked my mother if I could start going to Hebrew school. She found the nearest congregation, located in a neighboring county, and registered my brother and me for Sunday school classes in Jewish History and Hebrew. Also that year, I received a book of Bible stories from the mail order book club I belonged to. Suddenly a lot of things fell into place. I understood finally who the Jewish people were and who Jesus was. I also understood what it meant to believe in Him, and why I didn't.

The most important thing that happened when I moved to North Carolina was that I met Sarah, who became one of my best friends for the next six years. Sarah knew more about religion than I did, but was also being raised in a secular home. Her parents were actively atheists, while my mother was just apathetic toward religion.

Together, Sarah and I visited different churches to see what they were like. We would talk about what they preached, often laughing about them. One preacher talked about Jews as the stumbling block preventing Jesus's return to Earth. Seated in the back of the sanctuary at the end of the pew, it was all I could do not to stick out my foot and trip him as he walked up the aisle at the end of the service; Sarah stopped me.

There was one church with a lovely chapel with a huge

stained-glass window we liked to visit to pray or meditate in. Sometimes we attended the youth group at the Methodist church. That's right: I was the little Jewish girl at the Methodist Youth Fellowship. I also went to a Mormon youth group and a Young Life group at different points in my adolescence.

When I was twelve, our Jewish History teacher was giving us a lesson on the Messiah and the prophecies in Isaiah. He was explaining what the Bible had to say about what would happen when the Messiah came. I raised my hand to say that when the Messiah came, the Christians would think it was the Second Coming, so we would all be in agreement. The teacher said there was no Second Coming. I said *we* knew that, but the Christians would think it was the second time, so it would be the same. He said, no, they were wrong, so it couldn't be the same. I stopped arguing with him, but I knew he was being stubborn. I still think I was right. That attitude of arrogance toward the beliefs of others is why I stopped being Jewish in any religious sense, although I still retain a Jewish sense of identity.

Obviously, I was looking for something. By the time I was fourteen, I was certain I wasn't an atheist. I had taken the arguments denying the existence of God to their logical conclusion and realized there had to be something that was here first. That something was God. I didn't know then that I was following in the footsteps of such great philosophers as Aristotle and St. Thomas Aquinas. Of course, the weakness with that conclusion is that it doesn't define the nature of God, only God's existence. It is up to us to create God in our image, or so I've come to believe.

By the time Kevin and I married, I knew I wanted to belong to a community of believers, but I didn't know what community that was. I limited my search to Western religions, including Judaism. I felt pretty comfortable with Christianity, except for the divinity of Jesus. That's a pretty big "except."

When Kevin and I got involved with the Marriage Encounter movement, I had the chance to sit down with a Catholic priest and talk about what I believed. In return, he shared Catholic doctrine with me. Even my doubts didn't seem to be a problem, but merely part of the human search for understanding. Kevin and I started to study at one of the local parishes, and a little over a year later, we joined the Catholic Church.

I was very happy as a Catholic for twelve years. I taught CCD (Sunday School), led the church Brownie troop, played the guitar for the children's liturgies, and even helped with Vacation Bible School. The only thing that troubled me was my growing certainty that God was Our Mother, not Our Father. There seemed no place for the feminine face of God in Christianity as a whole, not just Catholicism. I started doing research on the ancient goddess religions, hoping to integrate some of those ideas into my private religious practice. Instead, I found a group of like-minded believers within the Unitarian Universalist Church.

There are those who argue Unitarian Universalism is not a religion, but rather a philosophy. I agree with them. UU's support each other in their individual search for truth and meaning, but we don't have a shared doctrine or dogma. Within a UU church, you will find many who identify themselves by hyphenated names: UU-Christians, UU-Jews, UU-Buddhists, UU-Hindus, UU-Pagans, UU-Humanists, etc. There are even UU-Atheists. I can think of no other spiritual community in which atheists would feel welcome. Unitarian Universalism has an umbrella large enough to shelter everyone who searches for truth, even if their paths lead them to very different conclusions.

It broke my heart to leave the Catholic Church, but I knew I no longer belonged there. I think now, having grown spiritually in the interim, I wouldn't have to leave under the same circumstances, but I didn't know that then. The best part about being a UU is I can remain a UU no matter where my spiritual journey takes me.

I now call myself an earth-centered atheist. I don't believe in any type of supreme being who 1) created everything, 2) is in control of everything, 3) is aware of our existence, and 4) is capable of intervening in our lives. That doesn't mean I reject the idea of our having a spiritual existence that transcends our physical life. Whatever that spark is that gives us intellect and awareness of our own being may continue to exist even when our bodies die. Or not. It's not something that is measurable by our current technology. There's no way to be certain, but I'm comfortable with that level of uncertainty. That's what "faith" is all about.

I specify being earth-centered because I agree with Henry Beston, an American author and naturalist, who observed "the adventure of the sun is the great natural drama by which we live, and not to have joy in it and awe of it, not to share in it, is to close a dull door on nature's sustaining and poetic spirit." Life on Earth would not be possible without the Sun. I don't worship the Sun, but I consider the dance of the heavens to be the events on Earth most worthy of celebration. Even birthdays celebrate completing a full circuit around the sun.

I'm sure you're wondering what this has to do with The French Court. The fact Michael and I were raised without any religion at all is attributable to Grandma Jean's rejection of religion after her father's death. Both Michael and I embarked on a personal search for God. My search started very young and ended when I became a member of a liberal, free-thinking denomination. Michael's search started at a later age and ended in a very conservative, evangelical denomination of Christianity. When I got sick enough to be hospitalized for depression, I started to hear the voice of a vengeful, judgmental God.

He spoke with Michael's voice.

THE DEEP WELL OF DEPRESSION

People often ask someone who has been depressed and suicidal how it is we can think about committing suicide and hurting all the people who love us. The first major depressive episode of my life happened when I was thirty-five.[1] It was 100% hormonally induced, which is somehow more acceptable and less "crazy" to other people than situational depression. It was diagnosed at the time as early peri-menopause, but turned out three years later to be poly cystic ovaries.

I fell so deep into depression that I underwent a slight temporary personality dissociation, so at times there were two or three personalities in my body. For example, I described feeling suicidal as "she's trying to kill us." This dissociation gave me an opportunity to observe what I was going through as an onlooker, even as I was going through it. So, for the edification of those readers who have no idea what depression feels like on the inside, and in support of those who know all too well, but don't

---

1. It is worth noting that my grandmother's first consultation with a psychiatrist happened when she was thirty-four. She got the same initial diagnosis. Probably coincidence.

have the words to say it, here's my description by analogy of that period in my life. Of course, it's only my description. It may not be true for anyone else, but I suspect parts of it are true for most of us who suffer from depression.

We all move through various circles in our lives. There's our work circle, our circle of friends, our church circle, and the circle of our family. There are the larger circles of our community and the smaller circle of our household. When depression starts to grow larger, the circles grow smaller, like moving through a funnel. The symptom is called something like losing interest in things that used to give pleasure, but it feels like the scope of your life is just smaller. There isn't as much room as there used to be. You drop out of activities because they are no longer part of the circle of your life. Friends disappear from your circle, but you don't really notice their absence. If the depression gets deep enough, eventually no one is left in your circle of existence except you. No matter how strong your faith once was, even God can't find you now. It can be lonely in the center by yourself, but at least you don't have to think about anyone else. No more decisions. You can just stay in bed and take care of yourself. What job? What family? What are they talking about?

At that point, it's as if you're tumbling down a well. Some instinct of self-preservation makes you reach out to grab one of the rusty metal rungs embedded in the sidewall of the well. You cling to the side of the well, panting and trembling. If you look up, there's a small dot of light overhead. If there's anyone else up there, you can't see or hear them. You know they're up there in the way you know the moon is up there, but you feel about as much connection to those people as you feel to the man in the moon.

You know you have to climb back up. You remember voices telling you that you have to climb. Your therapist. Your spouse. Your parents. Your colleagues. You know they are right, even though they are just voices. So many disembodied voices. It sure is a long way up. It would be so much easier to let go. You can only die once, and then the pain is over forever. Isn't it? There's no one else here in your small lonely circle who would be hurt if you let go. You know just how you would do it.

The siren song of death is strong in the deep dark well of depression. It takes tremendous strength not to give in and let go. Most of us make the decision to climb, rung by rung, slowly and painfully out of that pit. Sometimes you get tired of the climbing and you act foolish, leaning back and holding on with one hand or banging your head against the stone wall of the well. That would be the risk-taking behavior people with depression often do, or the self-injurious behaviors that serve to remind you you're alive even while you're trying to get back to the world of the living. When pain is the only thing you can feel, feeling it reminds you that you can still feel *something*. You're still alive.

The light from above grows ever brighter as you climb, and one day you can hear and see the people you remember loving. They're up there, ringing the opening to the well, looking down and cheering you on. Suddenly you feel something for someone other than yourself for the first time in what might have been forever. You realize you've been totally focused on yourself. At first you feel guilty and selfish and, paradoxically, you feel suicidal all over again. But you worked too hard to climb up from that well, and you're not going to let yourself fall back down. You suddenly find that if you bang your head against that brick wall or cut yourself, it *hurts*. You're finally able to accept help from your loved ones, so now when they reach a hand out to you, you gratefully grasp it and let them help you up.

Once you stand in the sunshine, you blink from the brightness. You're out of breath from the climb. Everyone gathers around to welcome you. You stand there, staring at the opening of the well from which you just emerged. You tremble, not knowing how or why you fell in, and knowing you could end up back in there at any time.

Knowing that is the real nightmare.

PERFECTIONISM

I used to believe perfectionists were made, not born. Demanding parents who were never satisfied turned other-wise normal children into perfectionists. My reasons for thinking so were the many times my mother had expected perfection from me and the way I had internalized her standards. I always judged myself more severely than anyone else did. Then Rebecca was born, and I had to change my way of thinking.

At three months old, most infants learn to roll from front to back. Sometimes, the first roll can be an accident, like when a turtle flips over. Eventually, the baby learns to roll over inten-tionally. Babies are usually absorbed in practicing this new skill. They don't particularly pay attention to who is watching them.

One afternoon, when Rebecca was three months old, the woman who cared for her during the day met me at the door with a puzzled expression on her face. Sue told me she thought Rebecca was rolling over, but she wasn't sure. Every time she put Rebecca in her crib, she placed her on her stomach, but when she went to get her, Rebecca was on her back. If she put Rebecca on a blanket on the floor on her stomach, she would just lie there, but if Sue left the room to get something, she would return to find Rebecca on her back. She thought Rebecca must be rolling over, but she couldn't ever catch her doing it. Sue couldn't believe a three-month-old baby would be waiting for her to leave the room. It was possible one of Sue's young children was rolling Rebecca over when Sue wasn't looking, but she didn't think so. It was a mystery.

The next day, Sue told me she had finally caught Rebecca in the act. She put her in the crib on her stomach and left the room, but hid behind the door. She watched Rebecca immediately roll over. Sue stepped out of her hiding place and exclaimed, "I gotcha!" Rebecca startled and then started to laugh. Sue told me the story shaking her head in amazement. She still couldn't believe a three-month-old had intentionally hidden rolling over from an adult.

I wasn't sure if I believed her conclusion either, but with the weight of other stories that have accumulated through the years, I believe it now. Rebecca never practiced walking skills: never took tentative steps, never practiced walking holding hands with adults, and only once, at eleven months, toddled on shaky legs from one parent to another. By twelve months old, she showed no interest in walking. One day, when Rebecca was thirteen months old, as I was setting down my briefcase and her diaper bag after work, I turned around to find her walking down the hall alone. I called her name, and she turned to me and laughed so hard she fell. She stood up without holding on to anything and walked back to me. She demonstrated the whole range of beginning walking skills within those few moments: walking, turning, and standing up without holding on. We'd never seen any of those skills before.

When Rebecca was around eighteen months old, we were at the library, flipping through a children's magazine. Rebecca started pointing to and naming letters of the alphabet. I asked her who taught her the letters. She said, "Big Bird." I had never heard her say the letters before, not even repeating them while watching television.

When she was two, I was writing the names of her classmates on Valentines Rebecca had made. She read almost all the names. Then she went on to read several common words. She thought it was a game. However, within a few weeks, realizing reading was a skill that was valued, Rebecca forgot how to read any words at all, including her own name. She didn't remember how to read until first grade.

When Rebecca was three, she picked up a pencil one day while she was waiting for me and wrote her name. She had never attempted to write her name before, but it was legible and clear.

In first grade, when Rebecca was finally ready to read, she moved immediately from reading individual words to reading chapter books. Because she has a learning disability that particularly affects her ability to process and sequence auditory information, she cannot understand phonics. Sounds of letters are a total mystery to her, even in adulthood. We didn't know how or when she had learned to read.

Rebecca tried to learn to play the violin through the Suzuki method, which was offered at her elementary school. The first year, when she was in first grade, was wonderful. Rebecca showed a natural gift for music and a good ear. She was one of the best in her class without ever practicing. The only problem was that during class performances, Rebecca would be too self-conscious to play.

In the second year, Rebecca found she couldn't be the best violinist in her class anymore without practicing. The problem with practicing is that in order to practice, you first have to acknowledge that what you are doing needs improvement. The concept of continuous improvement never resonated with Rebecca. She couldn't handle being less than perfect, so she couldn't practice. Without practicing, she couldn't be the best. She became a nervous wreck. She had to drop violin midyear.

The same thing eventually happened with drums and piano as well.

The one area where Rebecca was willing to practice was dance. Rebecca had always learned best when her whole body was involved, and dancing came as naturally to her as walking. One day, when she was in third grade, she came home from school excited about a science lesson on erosion. As Kevin and I watched, Rebecca danced around the living room, showing us the movement of the waves against the rocks and the wind weathering the cliffs. Kevin asked Rebecca if the dance was how the teacher had taught the lesson. "No," explained Rebecca. "That's how I understand it." Even so, Rebecca's self-consciousness often got in the way of her being able to perform in dance recitals until she was old enough to understand how to overcome her "invisible audience."

The imaginary invisible audience Rebecca carried around in her head is usually characteristic of adolescents. They feel they are constantly being judged by an unseen group of peers. Of course, for adolescents, the truth is each one of them is carrying around that imaginary audience; no one is looking at them. For Rebecca, though, she was carrying around that invisible audience even as young as two years old. Rebecca's audience always judged her harshly, and for them, Rebecca had to be perfect.

In high school, Rebecca wanted to learn to play golf. Her favorite relative, my father, played golf, and she wanted to be able to share that hobby with him. She took lessons at one of the local golf courses and worked hard to improve. However, she couldn't practice her swing in our yard. The backyard was where the dogs played and wasn't really suitable for golf practice. Rebecca couldn't stand the thought of being in the front yard where people might see her. It didn't matter that no one else would care; the mere fact someone *could* see her was enough to keep her from practicing. Again, her invisible audience prevented her from doing something she wanted to do.

As parents, we recognized very early in Rebecca's life that we were dealing with a perfectionist. We also realized that, contrary to our previous beliefs, some perfectionists are born and not made. Not only was Rebecca a perfectionist long before we could have turned her into one, but we actively did everything we could to counteract her tendency toward perfectionism. We stressed process over product, and effort over results. Let me give two examples that illustrate this pretty clearly.

Because Rebecca had trouble with both sounds and sequencing, spelling tests were a nightmare for her. She could hear the sounds that were in a word, but she had no idea what order they were in. When she misspelled a word, she would usually get all the right letters, but in the wrong order. One week, in fourth grade, I helped her study for her spelling test the next day, but she still earned a "D." She was very upset and expected to be punished, though we'd never punished her before for bad grades, nor praised her excessively for good ones. I asked her if she had studied for the test, knowing we had worked together on the list the night before. She tearfully nodded yes. I asked her if she had done her best on the test. Another nod. I told her if she did her best, then I was proud of her. She sniffled, we hugged, and that was it. I rewarded her for her effort, not for her results.

In contrast, in eighth grade, Rebecca and her partner won first place in the school science fair. Their project used what was at the time cutting edge technology that wowed the judges, but they hadn't done the research to support the project. Their teacher didn't think the project had much scientific merit. He told the two students and their parents that he had no choice but to give the students A's on their report cards—the promised incentive for winning—but he would not send the project on to the county level fair unless they did more work.

Kevin and I put Rebecca on electronic restriction (no computer, tv, etc.; that was her most hated punishment) over the Thanksgiving break until she completed the required work. She protested because she didn't care if the project went on to the next level of competition. We told her that was too bad; she had to do the work anyway because it should have been done in the first place. She said it wasn't fair to require more work, since she'd gotten first place and an "A." We told her it was about effort, not results, and always had been. Rebecca chose not to do the work; the restriction lifted at the end of the holiday weekend.

Kevin and I tried as hard as we could to help Rebecca overcome the influence of her all-powerful invisible audience. I don't think we were very successful. As an adult, Rebecca struggles with Rejection Sensitive Dysphoria, essentially a misperception of and overreaction to apparent criticism. It took until Rebecca was about twenty-one for her to realize we were not the source of her perfectionism. I guess there's some comfort in knowing that if we couldn't prevent or cure her perfectionism, at least we weren't getting blamed for it.

HEALING

I started seeing a therapist in 1988 because of stress at work. It was a short-term intervention as part of that employer's Employee Assistance Program. I gained the tools I needed to cope with the immediate problem that had arisen. I didn't gain any insight into my larger problems, but the counselor recommended I pursue additional therapy when I could.

When the next school year started, I was in graduate school and went to the university counseling center for help. After an intake interview, I was offered a spot in a therapy group. I attended faithfully. For the first semester, I was more willing to speak up in support of others than to share much about myself. That changed the day one of the two counselors leading the group wore black gloves.

I had an uncomfortable reaction to seeing someone indoors with black gloves on and asked if she could remove them. My request was granted, but then I had to explain why the gloves had bothered me enough to make me speak up. For the first time in group, I shared the bare bones story of The French Court. No one judged me for having had such a horrible childhood. They didn't particularly judge my family. Although I had been embarrassed telling Grandma Jean's story to relative strangers, that feeling soon faded as I realized I was in a safe place.

Eventually, I was comfortable enough to share problems that were more personal. I was frustrated I couldn't get things done. I described feeling weighed down by an inertia I was incapable of overcoming. Several voices at once said, "Depression!" I assumed being depressed meant feeling sad, so I stereotypically responded that I wasn't sad. I was quickly given an education on depression by my fellow group members, as well as the group leaders.

People say, "I'm depressed" when they mean they are extremely sad. A person with depression isn't necessarily depressed and vice versa. Depression isn't an emotion; depression is a pervasive mood that makes the patient feel unable to cope with the world as it is. Feeling weighed down and unable to break through inertia are hallmark descriptions of depression. After the session, the leaders asked me if I wanted to be evaluated for depression. I accepted their offer.

I met with the psychiatrist who provided services to the university. He gave me the Minnesota Multiphasic Personality Inventory, a self-reported inventory that is used to diagnose mental health conditions in adults. Later that same day, I had to fill out a similar parent-reported inventory for my four-year-old daughter. The results showed I had depression and Rebecca had a "depressive personality." I started individual therapy with one of the group leaders, continuing to see her on a private basis after I graduated.

Since the diagnosis had come about from a discovery in therapy, rather than because of a crisis, I didn't see a reason to try medication. Two years later, I was dealing with a lot of stress at work, mostly triggered by a violent student and insufficient administrative support. I went back to the same psychiatrist and asked for something to deal with the anxiety. I was surprised at how well the medication worked. I returned to the doctor and asked for antidepressants, just to see what would happen. My reaction to taking Prozac felt nearly miraculous. I can't really describe what changed, except I seemed better able to handle the minor turbulence of human existence. I became more resilient.

I continued working with Grace, my therapist, for several years. My concerns about parenting were a large part of our conversations. I knew by then that I had been severely neglected as a child. I was angry with my mother for the things she hadn't done that, as a mother myself, I knew good mothers did. Grace encouraged me to share my upset with my mother, but I didn't see any value in confronting her or even writing a letter I didn't intend to mail. Mother wouldn't have understood, and would undoubtedly have been hurt and defensive. I didn't think an apology from her would be particularly healing. There was no action she could take that would repair the damage she had done. Instead, I kept my feelings to myself, though I shared them with my husband. I withdrew and kept my mother at arm's length during the years I was trying to reconcile an adult relationship with her with the neglect I had suffered as a child.

The single most important thing that came out of my sessions with Grace was when she recommended that I parent Rebecca the way I wished my mother had parented me. I translated that into actively healing myself by being the mother Rebecca deserved. I know I wasn't anything close to perfect, but in trying to do my best for my own daughter, I helped my mother's daughter, too.

I remained in therapy from 1988 to 2012. Over the course of those years, and over the course of numerous weekly or biweekly sessions with therapists in North Carolina, Florida, Illinois, and Maryland, I was able to understand that I didn't need to blame myself for the things that went wrong in my life and relationships, especially if I knew I had given my best. Even when my best wasn't good enough.

With that insight, I was able to forgive my mother as well. I might perceive reasons she could have known and done better, but she, too, had done the best she was capable of doing. I slowly thawed our relationship, and grew to love my mother for the warm and talented person she was. She was the person who instilled in me a volunteer ethic of sharing the best I had to offer with my community. I, in turn, modeled that ethic to Rebecca, who is now a social worker focused on community organizing around the issue of fair housing. I looked forward to weekly phone calls with my mother, and found myself caring deeply about her wellbeing. She never knew I had withdrawn, but she noticed the increase in affection as we got older. I am grateful that by the time Mother died in 2018, I loved her enough to mourn for her. I still miss her every day.

* * *

THERE WERE a few lapses in therapy when I was between therapists in a new location, but they were lapses of months, not years. For the most part, I knew I needed that support and made it a priority. My suicide attempt, in March, 2010, came when I was between therapists. By October, 2012, I felt secure enough to move halfway around the world to China, even knowing I wouldn't have access to mental health care.

I don't speak Chinese, although I picked up a few words and phrases during the three years I lived there. I was puzzled that my neighbors seemed to like me, though they mostly couldn't communicate with me. When a bilingual friend was able to talk with my neighbors, they universally described me as "kind." I'd never seen myself that way. I wondered why I could get along with others better when they could only judge my behavior, not my words. I wondered what was wrong with me.

I resumed therapy in Alaska, in 2017, after my service dog died. Cody's death was traumatic for me because I had had to nurse him on his deathbed for five days, a task I wasn't prepared for in any sense. I needed the help of a therapist to process what had happened. As we continued working together, I shared my newfound concerns about possibly being autistic. My therapist conducted an interview assessment and concluded I had an Autism Spectrum Disorder. She later stopped visiting our island, so I again stopped therapy. I resumed after I moved to Oregon, but that was during the Covid-19 pandemic. I only saw my new therapist once in person; other than that, our sessions were online.

Most of my therapy since resuming in 2020, and even after moving back to Alaska in December, 2023, has been about what my autism means. I've examined much of my past to see if there were signs of autism. There's the story of my apparent personality change when my brother was born when I was sixteen months old. I sucked my thumb until I was ten years old. I only stopped because I slammed the finger in a one-inch-thick steel door, and it hurt too much for me to suck it. By the time my thumb healed, the habit was broken.

I remember hiding under the dining room table when my stepsister played the radio too loud. I remember sitting in the closet, the door closed, stroking the fur collar of a jacket over and over. My favorite toy—and the only one I still own from my childhood—was an abacus. I remember being scolded because I had deformed my shoes by always walking on tiptoe. I remember being told regularly to close my mouth; not to stop talking, but to stop sitting with my mouth ajar. I also remember my childhood obsession with astronomy. I got a telescope for my ninth birthday. I was ten years old at the time of the first moon landing. My mother's adult friends who had come over to watch the event with us were surprised at my knowledge of the solar system.

My behavior had always been odd, but it wasn't a problem until I moved from New York to North Carolina at ten. Suddenly, I was not only odd, but I was a Jewish Yankee in a small, southern town filled with Baptists. I was grateful there was another girl in my sixth-grade class who was also different, having lived in England prior to moving to North Carolina. We found each other because of our differences from the others, but we were bound together by our many shared interests. Sarah remained one of my best friends until she moved away during high school.

By the time I started junior high, I had adopted "weird" as my mask. I was an artsy kid, even at ten. I had started acting lessons before leaving New York. I had gotten a guitar for my tenth birthday, and being "the girl with the guitar" was a major part of my identity. Artsy and weird fit well together, especially once I started socializing with the drama majors who frequented our home.

My autism was on full display, if anyone had been looking. Given the definitions of autism at the time, though, I probably wouldn't have been picked up even if someone had been looking. If my younger self were attending today's schools, I would definitely be noticed, no matter how well I masked. I was a clumsy child, uncoordinated and slow to acquire physical skills; I couldn't skip until fifth grade. My fine motor coordination was behind my classmates, though I mostly caught up by adulthood. I lacked social skills. I was a picky eater. I sometimes rocked in class without realizing I was doing it. Ditto for thumb-sucking. I also sucked my hair. Plus the toe-walking. I might not be placed in a special class in a twenty-first century American elementary school, since I was bright and highly verbal, but I would certainly be identified and probably have an IEP for support.

I've also looked at my past relationships, both personal and professional, for clues about why I was never successful as a teacher. My teaching itself wasn't a problem, but my interactions with colleagues always seemed to get me in trouble. My supervisors would talk to me about it, but they could never pick out exactly what it was I had done or said. It was like an aura hanging over me, but nothing anyone could define. Now I know that I'm very autistic. Even though I'm generally able to function in society, I am unable to work because I can't meet the social demands of being employed. I have been receiving disability payments since 2017. I can't help but wonder whether, if I had been identified in childhood and had received the kinds of interventions that are now available, I would have fulfilled all the promise within me.

I still see a therapist. I had an acute illness in 2021 that led to a nine-day hospitalization with an initial diagnosis of dementia. The hospital called my daughter to tell her I would never recover and to look for memory care for me. I recovered—mostly. I have lost some abilities permanently, but testing shows my recovery is stable. I won't regain the abilities I've lost, but at least I'm not continuing to decline. I'm developing coping skills for having almost no short-term memory and for having extreme difficulty with learning new things, among other problems.

I will probably always be in therapy as I try to cope with my life as it is and as it will become as I age. I am thankful to live in a time when seeking therapy is acceptable and socially supported. I wish Grandma Jean had had similar access to help when her problems first appeared. I wonder how my life could have been different if my family had secured treatment for Grandma Jean instead of creating The French Court. I wonder how different all our lives might have been.

GOODBYE, GRANDMA JEAN

W e got the word that Kevin's grandmother had died on a Monday in July, 2003. Rebecca had only met her great-grandmother twice, once when she was six and Kevin's grandparents had driven cross-country to visit their grandchildren, and once when she was sixteen, and we had attended Great-grandma's hundredth birthday party in Oregon. I didn't think Rebecca would be very upset about her death, but I wanted to make sure she knew about it. Rebecca had just finished her first semester at Florida State and was working as a counselor at a Girl Scout camp in North Carolina, the same one she'd attended as a child. I called the office and let the director know what had happened, asking her to please tell Rebecca as soon as possible. No, I assured the director, family leave to attend the funeral wouldn't be necessary.

As it happened, within moments of hanging up the phone, the director was confronted with an emergency and forgot to give Rebecca the message. Instead, Rebecca learned the news via an email from Kevin two days later. I was furious she hadn't been told in person, but there was no need to call the camp to complain. The incident was over.

The following Monday morning, the phone rang at 7:00. It was Aunt Mary. Grandma Jean had died. My mother was on a cruise ship. Did I know how to contact her? I sleepily stumbled downstairs and placed a satellite call to the ship to give my mother the news. Then I called the camp to ask the director to tell Rebecca her great-grandmother had died. The director started to apologize for being so late in relaying the message, but said she had already given it to Rebecca.

"No, different great-grandmother," I said.

She asked, "What do you people do to your grandmothers?"

I realized Rebecca might be hit a little harder by this death. Rebecca had never known Grandma Jean in full bitch mode. Her life had never been disrupted by Grandma Jean's OCD. Rebecca had been the last girl to be the apple of Grandma's eye. Whenever we were coming for a visit, Grandma Jean would buy a box of animal crackers for Rebecca out of her meager funds. To Rebecca, Grandma Jean was a sweet old lady who gave her cookies and sang songs with her.

Rebecca wanted to say goodbye to Grandma Jean. Although Orthodox Jews do not embalm their dead, our family is not Orthodox. Grandma Jean was being embalmed in preparation for transport to New York for burial beside Grandpa Bob. The Girl Scout camp was only about an hour from the funeral home where Grandma Jean had been taken. Rebecca contacted the funeral home and made arrangements for a private viewing. She drove herself from the camp to the funeral home to say goodbye.

Even though there was a dutiful burial service in New York, that hastily arranged viewing at the funeral home when my daughter said a tearful goodbye to Grandma Jean was probably the only time she was truly mourned.

MEDIUM

I've been aware of being what most people call "psychic"
since I was about twelve years old. I'm not interested in
trying to convince people that such phenomena are
different from or separate from the mental illnesses I've
described in this book. Maybe they are just a different manifestation of the same thing. That's not my debate. Whether psychic
visions are true spiritual entities or merely parts of our own
personalities doesn't matter to me. I don't have a dog in that
fight.

Neither is this a book about the paranormal, so I'm not planning to describe all the things that have happened that have
shown me I am in touch with a world that is not normally acces-
sible to us. My usual guide in this world, at least since his death,
is my father's father, Grandpa Irving. Again, I don't care if I'm
seeing the real Grandpa Irving in my dreams or if he's just a
representation of some part of myself. He still functions as a
conduit to knowledge I'm not otherwise aware of.

Grandpa Irving was a tailor; I often sense him watching me
while I sew. Other than that, he sometimes guides me through
dreams. On rare occasions, especially when I have a specific

question for him, he will talk to me and show me things. Surprisingly, he has talked to me more than once about Grandma Jean.

I say that it is surprising, but not because he didn't know Grandma Jean. He knew her well enough, since they were in-laws to each other's children and grandparents to the same children. However, they also hated each other in life. I wouldn't expect him to give a proverbial rat's ass about what happened to her after her death, yet he started talking to me about it well in advance, some twelve years before the event.

The first time I dreamed about what life after death would be like for Grandma Jean, Grandpa Irving showed me an image of my mother and my aunt hearing the news of their mother's death. Both were glad to be rid of her. In fact, they were down-right gleeful in my dream. My brother Michael, who by then was an evangelical Christian, believed she would be burning in Hell because she had not been saved. Anita and Mary thought she deserved to burn in Hell for what she had done to her family.

Grandpa took me to see the afterlife. In my dream, I realized that once Grandma Jean shed her physical body, she wouldn't be mentally ill anymore. She would be a purely spiritual being. She would be Jean the way God had created Jean to be, and God's Jean was perfect.

That was the message my dream self tried to carry back to the dream images of Anita, Mary, and Michael. None of them would believe me. In my dream, I tried to talk to them individually and together, but they all had their own reasons for believing God couldn't mean to spare Jean from Hell.

About four months after Grandma Jean died, I asked Grandpa Irving in a dream how she was doing. He didn't answer me directly, but he showed me a vision of the torments she was suffering. It wasn't that she was in Hell as the popular mythology would have it. No demons with pitchforks were torturing her in a fiery pit. Rather, now that she was God's perfect Jean, she was able to look back at her life with perfect clarity. She could see all the damage she had caused her family and all her descendants. She was suffering the knowledge of what she had done. I asked Grandpa Irving if there was anything I could do to help Grandma Jean. How could I give her peace? He said I could forgive her and pray for her. I can't forgive her for what she did until I understand it. Perhaps this book is the first step.

Requiescat in pace, Avia.

ACKNOWLEDGMENTS

This book was challenging to write both because it is so intensely personal and because of the format I chose to use. I needed the support and encouragement of many people in order to complete the manuscript after letting it sit for twenty years.

Thanks as always to my editor, Lindz McLeod, whose suggestions helped me flesh out details and make the story more coherent.

Thank you to my brilliant cover designer, Emilija Rakić, of Emily's World of Design, who took my nebulous ideas and made them real.

I recruited several alpha readers while working on the first draft of *The French Court*. Those readers gave me feedback that helped me finish writing the story of my family. Thank you to Evelyn Maurakis Seabold, Wanda Frazier, Amy Brener, Lori Weinke-Leger, and Anne Celeste Dowling.

Thank you, too, to the fellow authors who read the manuscript when it was complete and offered feedback: Judy Lannon; Joseph Taiwo, of Beta Brilliance; and Rebecca E. Schmuck, of The Write Author. Your feedback was invaluable.

ABOUT THE AUTHOR

Lauren is a former teacher, having started in Special Education before transitioning to become an English Language Arts/English as a Second Language teacher. She is fascinated by everything having to do with language and linguistics. She can explain arcane points of grammar with enthusiasm and joy, possibly a consequence of her Autism Spectrum Disorder. Although teaching is rarely seen as a glamorous job, Lauren has had the pleasure of teaching in places that people often consider exotic, like China and Alaska. Lauren lives near Fairbanks, Alaska, along with Shadow, a grumpy poodle, Shenanigans, a Lab mix, and Sir-the-Cat, who runs the household.

Lauren's previous books include **Cody: The Extraordinary Life of an Ordinary Dog** and **Satan's Therapist**. Visit Lauren's website for more information: https://laurenhenrybrehm.com/.